NSO OLYMPIAD WORKBOOK 2

SOF NATIONAL SCIENCE OLYMPIAD

2017-18

By

Anil Ahlawat

MTG Learning Media (P) Ltd.

New Delhi | Gurgaon

Revised Edition : 2017

ISBN 978–93–86379–85–6

Corporate Office : Plot 99, Sector 44 Institutional area, Gurgaon -122 003 (HR) Telefax : 0124-6601200

Regd. Office : 406, Taj Apt., Ring Road, Adjacent Safdarjung Hospital, New Delhi - 110 029.

Web : mtg.in Email : info@mtg.in

Visit www.mtg.in for

- **Last 5 years' papers of NSO**
- **Level 1 and level 2 preparation material**

CONTENTS

There are different types of plants. Some are big and some are small. They are of different shapes and sizes.

Trees

These are big and tall plants. They have hard and strong stems. They may have branches or not. Examples are *peepal*, *jamun* and coconut.

A

D

Climbers

These plants have weak stems. They cannot grow straight. They need support to stand and grow straight. Examples are pea, bean and money plant.

B

Shrubs

These are much smaller than trees. These have many branches growing close to the ground. Examples are China rose, cotton and mehendi.

Herbs

These are very smalls plants. They have soft stems. Examples are mint, spinach and rice.

C

Creepers

These plants have weak stems. They grow along the ground. Examples are bottlegourd and watermelon

E

Plants have many parts like stem, leaves, flowers, fruits and roots. Each of them play important roles.

We get many things from plants :

- **Plants give us food like** fruits, vegetables, nuts, cereals and pulses.
- **Plants give us fibres :** Cotton plant and jute plant.
- **Plants give us wood :** Teak, pine and bamboo.
- **Plants give us oil :** Groundnut, sunflower and mustard.
- **Plants give us paper, gum and rubber :** Bamboo, Acacia (keekar) tree.
- **Plants give us coffee, tea and sugar :** Cocoa, tea plant, sugarcane.

CHAPTER 1

Plants

Test Skills

- *Types of plants*
- *Parts of a plant and their functions*
- *Food and other things we get from plants*

1. **Plants give us foodgrains. What are the examples of such grains?**
   (A) Wheat and rice
   (B) Maize and barley
   (C) Gram and pulses
   (D) All of these

2. **We get gum from the ______________ tree.**
   (A) Acacia
   (B) Oak
   (C) Bamboo
   (D) Jasmine

3. **The stem pulp of the plant shown here is used to make**

   (A) Rubber (B) Gum (C) Paper (D) Oil.

4. **Select the pair that is similar to the one given in box based on their type.**

   (A) Basil : China rose
   (B) Bottle gourd : Grapevine
   (C) Money plant : Pea
   (D) Mehendi : Watermelon

5. **We get oil from all of the following plants except_______________.**

(A) 

(B) 

(C) 

(D) 

6. **Select the odd one out, based on the edible part.**

(A) 

(B) 

(C) 

(D) 

7. **Refer to the given picture of a plant with its few parts labelled. The part_________ is essential for the plant because in its absence it cannot produce seed.**

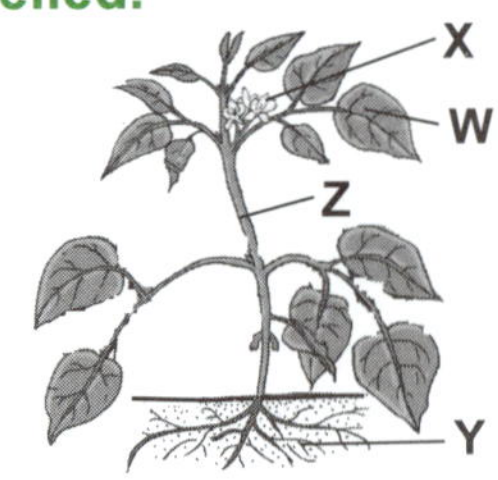

(A) W

(B) X

(C) Y

(D) Z

8. **Which of the following figures correctly shows the movement of water in the plant?**

(A) 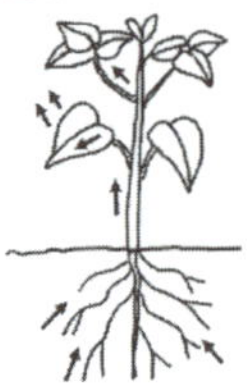

(B) 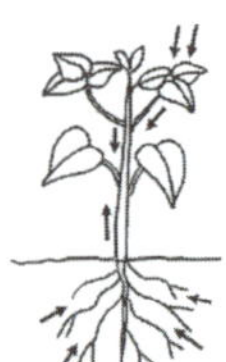

(C) 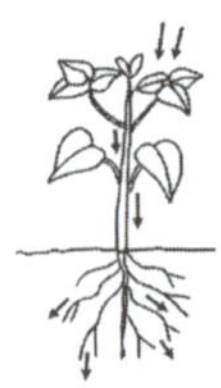

(D) 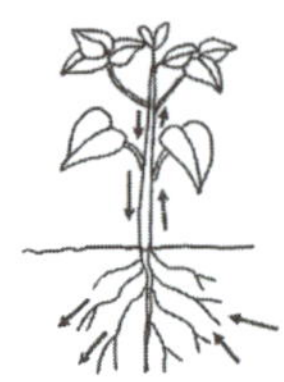

9. **Sameer describes a plant that he has seen in a field. Identify the plant.**

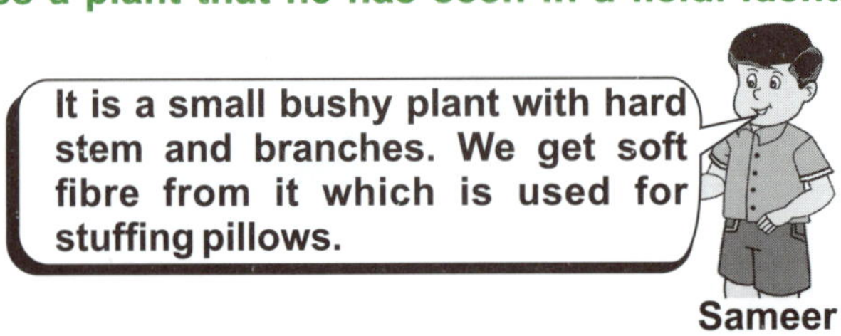

(A) Jute plant (B) Cotton plant (C) Coconut plant (D) Money plant

10. **What is the characteristic of the plant whose product is shown below?**

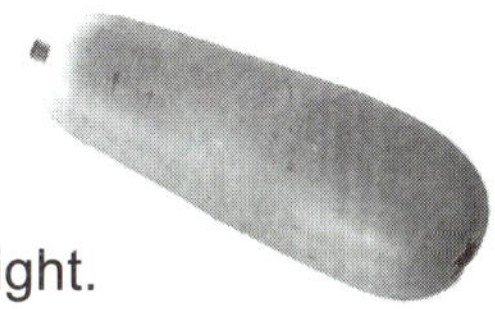

(A) The plant is small with woody stem.
(B) The plant is small with soft stem.
(C) The plant has weak stem and it grows along the ground.
(D) The plant has weak stem and needs support to grow upright.

11. **How is a young plant different from an adult plant?**
(A) The adult plant has roots but the young plant does not.
(B) The adult plant has a stem but the young plant does not.
(C) The adult plant has flowers but the young plant does not.
(D) The adult plant does not need air but the young plant does.

12. **Different plants live for different time periods. Arrange the following plants starting from the plant with shortest life span.**

Banyan	Rice	Rose
1	2	3

(A) 3, 2, 1 (B) 2, 3, 1
(C) 1, 2, 3 (D) 3, 1, 2

13. **What will happen to a plant if we remove all the leaves from it?**
(A) It will stop making food.
(B) It cannot stand upright on the ground.
(C) It will stop transporting food and water to all other parts.
(D) It will stop absorbing nutrients and water from the soil.

14. **Select the INCORRECT statement out of the following.**
(A) Rubber is made from stem juice of a shrub.
(B) Paper is made from stem pulp of a tree.
(C) Sugar is made from stem juice of a grass.
(D) Mustard oil is obtained from seeds of a herb.

15. **Study the given flow chart and select the option that correctly fills the empty spaces d and e.**

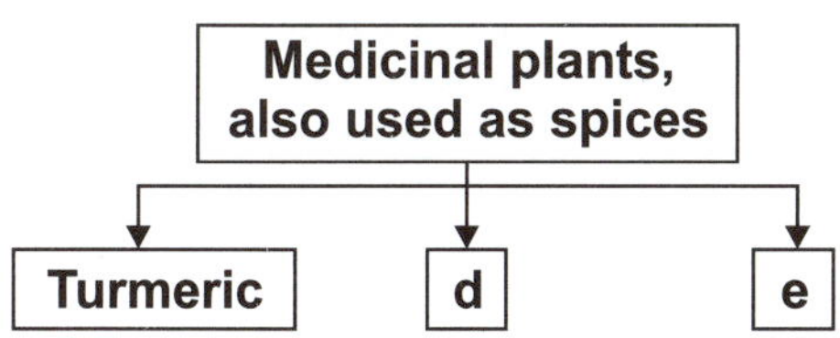

(A) Cinnamon and Neem (B) Clove and Mustard
(C) Tulsi and Cocoa (D) Cardamom and Almond

Achievers Section (HOTS)

16. What are the similarities between the plants bearing the flowers as shown?

(a) They have weak stems.
(b) They have woody stems.
(c) They produce seeds.
(d) They grow along the ground.

(A) (a) and (b) only
(B) (a) and (d) only
(C) (b) and (c) only
(D) (a), (b) and (c) only

17. Study the given figure. Which of the following best represents X and Y?

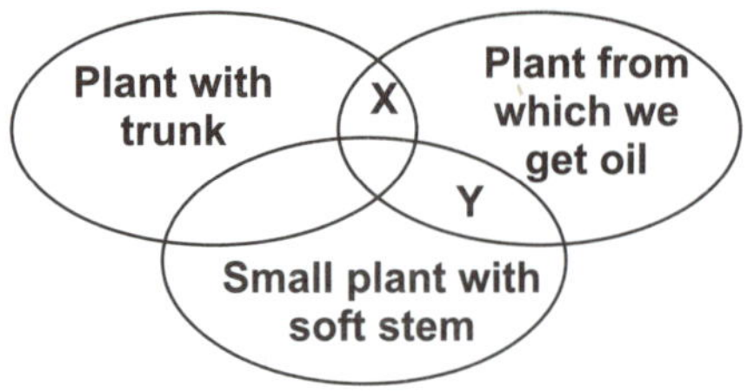

(A) X – Mustard, Y – Sunflower
(B) X – Coconut, Y – Sunflower
(C) X – Sunflower, Y – Groundnut
(D) X – Groundnut, Y – Mustard

18. Study the given flow chart. Which of the following is correct regarding this?

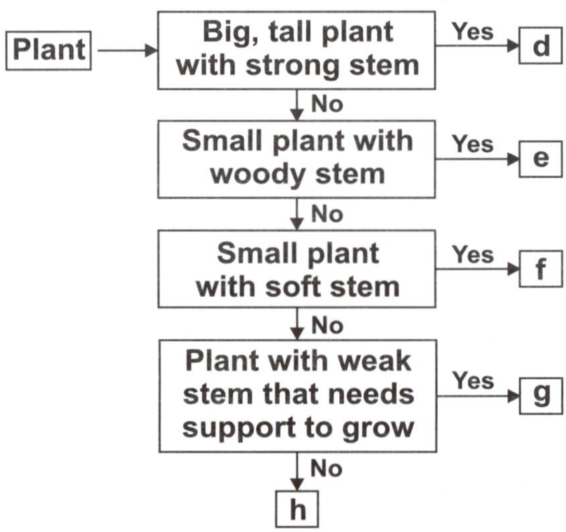

(A) g is a creeper and f is a climber.
(B) d represents coriander plant.
(C) e is a shrub.
(D) h represents coconut tree.

19. **The given figure shows a plant with its parts labelled as P, Q, R and S. Which of the following is correct regarding this?**

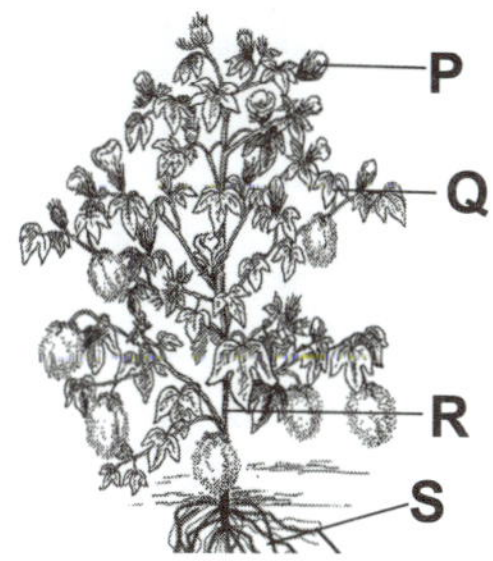

(A) We eat R of groundnut.
(B) We eat P of broccoli.
(C) We eat S of cabbage.
(D) We eat Q of potato.

20. **Refer to the given word chop table. Select the boxes that will give answers to the following questions.**
   a. **Name of the plant whose fruit is used to get oil.**
   b. **Name of the plant part that is eaten in radish.**

1 COC	2 RO	3 NIP	4 ON
5 TUR	6 ONI	7 ICK	8 LE
9 ROO	10 OF	11 NUT	12 SUG
13 OT	14 COCO	15 AF	16 AR

	a	b
(A)	6, 4	12, 16
(B)	14, 11	2, 13
(C)	1, 7	9, 10
(D)	5, 3	8, 15

☺☺☺

Darken your choice with HB Pencil

1.	Ⓐ Ⓑ Ⓒ Ⓓ	6.	Ⓐ Ⓑ Ⓒ Ⓓ	11.	Ⓐ Ⓑ Ⓒ Ⓓ	16.	Ⓐ Ⓑ Ⓒ Ⓓ
2.	Ⓐ Ⓑ Ⓒ Ⓓ	7.	Ⓐ Ⓑ Ⓒ Ⓓ	12.	Ⓐ Ⓑ Ⓒ Ⓓ	17.	Ⓐ Ⓑ Ⓒ Ⓓ
3.	Ⓐ Ⓑ Ⓒ Ⓓ	8.	Ⓐ Ⓑ Ⓒ Ⓓ	13.	Ⓐ Ⓑ Ⓒ Ⓓ	18.	Ⓐ Ⓑ Ⓒ Ⓓ
4.	Ⓐ Ⓑ Ⓒ Ⓓ	9.	Ⓐ Ⓑ Ⓒ Ⓓ	14.	Ⓐ Ⓑ Ⓒ Ⓓ	19.	Ⓐ Ⓑ Ⓒ Ⓓ
5.	Ⓐ Ⓑ Ⓒ Ⓓ	10.	Ⓐ Ⓑ Ⓒ Ⓓ	15.	Ⓐ Ⓑ Ⓒ Ⓓ	20.	Ⓐ Ⓑ Ⓒ Ⓓ

Domestic Animals

- Pet animals and farm animals are called domestic animals.
- Some of them give us food like milk, eggs and meat.
- Some animals give us silk, wool and leather. Leather is made from the skin of dead animals.
- Some animals help us to carry load.
- Some animals look after our houses.

Cow gives us milk.

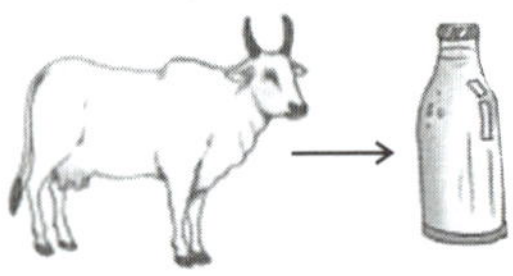

We get silk from silkworm.

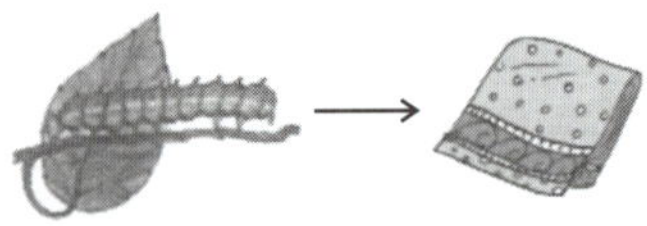

Hen, duck and geese give us eggs.

The fur on the body of the sheep is used to make wool.

Animals	Sounds
Tiger	Growl
Lion	Roar
Elephant	Trumpet
Horse	Neigh
Cow	Moo
Sheep	Baa
Monkey	Chatter
Dog	Bark
Cat	Meow
Duck	Quack
Crow	Caw
Donkey	Bray

Wild Animals

- These animals live in the jungles.
- Tigers, zebras, giraffes, bears, dear, owls and snakes are some wild animals.
- Wild animals live in different kinds of homes.
- Bear lives in caves. Birds make nests to lay eggs and to keep their nestlings safe. Animals like moles, rats, mongooses, snakes and rabbits live in holes in the ground. Some animals like elephant, gorillas and monkeys wander in the jungle.

- Some animals eat plants. Some eat the flesh of other animals.
- Young ones of different animals are known by different names *e.g.*, baby of cow is called calf, baby of kangaroo is called joey, etc.
- We must protect animals and their homes.

CHAPTER

2

Animals

Test Skills

- ❑ ***Domestic and wild animals***
- ❑ ***Eating habits of animals***
- ❑ ***Young ones of animals***
- ❑ ***Care of animals***
- ❑ ***Habitats of animals***
- ❑ ***Sounds of animals***
- ❑ ***Things we get from animals***

1. Which of these activities we should NOT do?

(A)  (B)  (C)  (D) All of these

2. Select the correct match out of the following.

(A) Tiger – Growl (B) Elephant – Trumpet
(C) Monkey – Chatter (D) All of these

3. ___________ is the name for the baby animal shown here.

(A) Joey
(B) Lamb
(C) Kid
(D) Infant

4. **Moo, Moo, where are you? Come to me I will give tasty_______ to you.**

Select the option that correctly fills the blank in the given statement.

(A) Leather (B) Egg (C) Milk (D) Oil

5. **Select the option that can complete the given table.**

Hole	Snake
X	Pigeon
Coop	Y

	X	Y
(A)	Burrow	Goat
(B)	Nest	Sparrow
(C)	Nest	Hen
(D)	Kennel	Goat

6. **Select the odd one on the basis of habitat.**

(A)  (B)  (C)  (D) 

7. **Select the habit, that we should NOT follow.**
   (A) Throwing stones at animals
   (B) Overloading the load carrying animals
   (C) Tying firecrackers on the tail of stray animals
   (D) All of these

8. **Ravi was asked to make four groups each with three animals which are useful to humans in a similar way. But he made a mistake. Select the option with mistake.**
   (A) Sheep, Yak, Rabbit
   (B) Cow, Goat, Buffalo
   (C) Hen, Duck, Goose
   (D) Elephant, Mule, Crocodile

9. **Which of the following statements is correct?**
   (A) Grass-eating animals have strong and broad back teeth to grind their food.
   (B) Flesh-eating animals have pointed teeth to tear the flesh.
   (C) Some animals have sharp front teeth both in upper and lower jaw to break open fruits and nuts.
   (D) All of these

10. **Select the option which on unscrambling gives the name of the home of dog.**
    (A) ENLKNE (B) YTS (C) ESBLTA (D) EHVI

11. **In the given diagram, what would giraffe be called?**

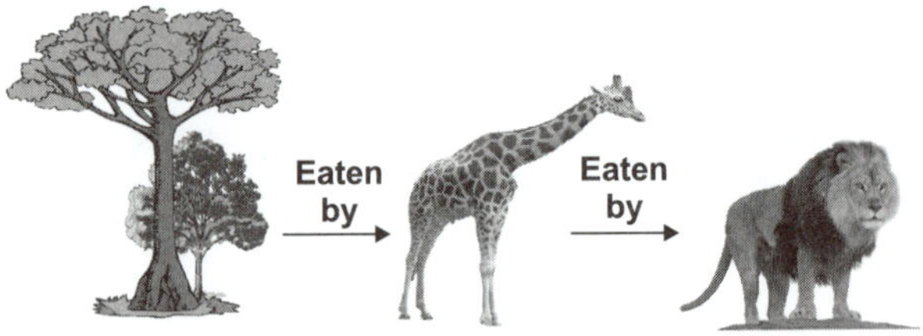

   (A) Prey animal
   (B) Endangered animal
   (C) Pet animal
   (D) Domestic animal

12. I'd love to ride a zebra
And stroke a lion's mane
Or race beside a cheetah
..................?..................

Which of the following will most correctly complete the given rhyme?

(A) If only they were in cage!
(B) If only they could be scared!
(C) If only they were tamed!
(D) None of these

13. **Select the option that correctly matches the objects shown here with the animals from which we get them.**

(A) 1–Yak, 3–Goat
(B) 2–Camel, 3–Sheep
(C) 2–Crocodile, 3–Silkworm
(D) 1–Sheep, 2–Mule

14. **Starting from the first letter, strike out every alternate letter in the given options and select the one that gives name of young one of the animal shown here.**

(A) R L S A U M A B B
(B) M C N A C L P F Q
(C) A K S I T D L
(D) U C V U X B Z

15. **Match column I with column II and select the correct option.**

	Column I		Column II
(a)	Camel	1.	King of the jungle
(b)	Cheetah	2.	Tallest land animal
(c)	Giraffe	3.	Largest land animal
(d)	Elephant	4.	Ship of the desert
(e)	Lion	5.	Fastest land animal

(A) (a) – 2, (b) – 1, (c) – 5, (d) – 4, (e) – 3
(B) (a) – 2, (b) – 5, (c) – 1, (d) – 3, (e) – 4
(C) (a) – 4, (b) – 5, (c) – 2, (d) – 3, (e) – 1
(D) (a) – 4, (b) – 5, (c) – 2, (d) – 1, (e) – 3

Achievers Section (HOTS)

16. **Study the given diagrams showing two aquariums. Vartika wants to find out if over crowding affects the animals living in an aquarium. In order to test the same, which of the following should she keep the same in both aquariums?**

(a) Number of fish (b) Amount of water (c) Size of tanks (d) Type of fish

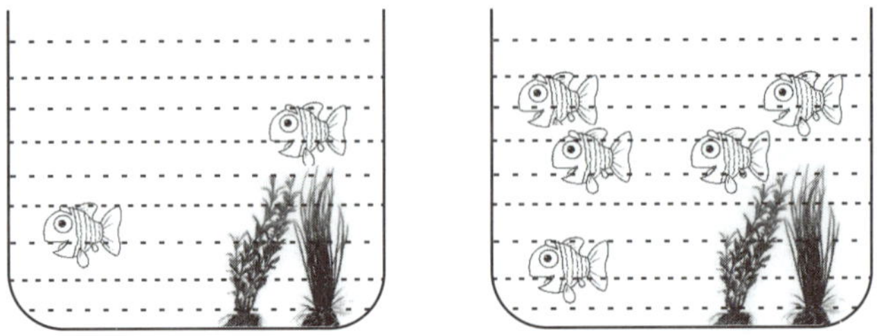

(A) (a) and (b) only
(B) (c) and (d) only
(C) (b), (c) and (d) only
(D) (a), (b), (c) and (d)

17. **Study the given classification chart. Where should (1) peacock and (2) louse be placed?**

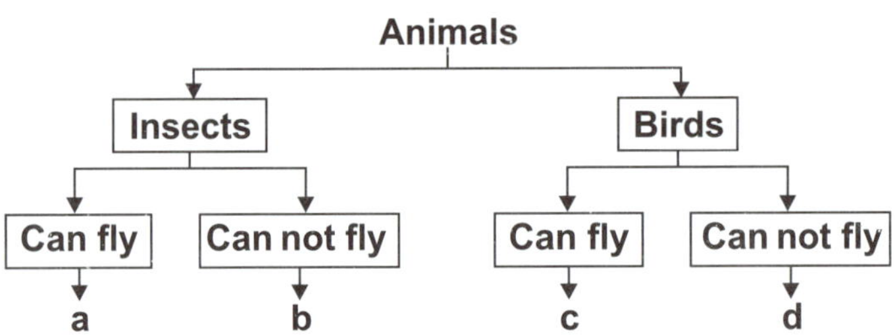

(A) (1) – d, (2) – b
(B) (1) – b, (2) – d
(C) (1) – c, (2) – b
(D) (1) – c, (2) – a

18. **Study the given figure and select the correct option regarding it.**

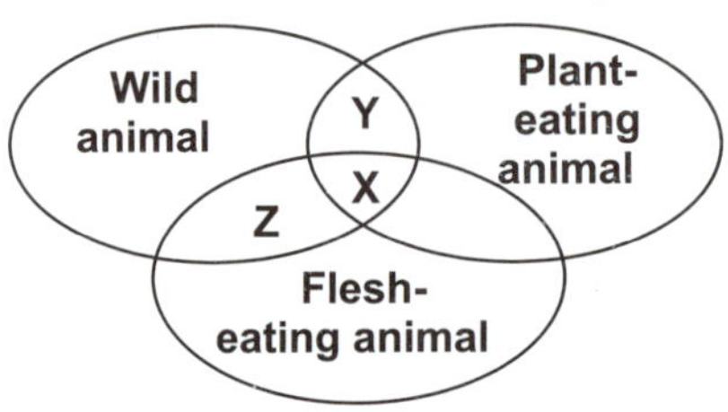

(A) X represents bear.
(B) Y represents zebra.
(C) Z represents lion.
(D) All of these

19. What are X and Y in the given rhyme?

Said the 'X' to the 'Y'
Good gracious! How you hop!
Over the field and in the water too,
As if you would never stop!
My life is a bore in this hasty pond,
And I long to go out in the world beyond.
I wish I could hop like you!'
Said the 'X' to the 'Y'.

	X	Y
(A)	Hen	Horse
(B)	Camel	Rabbit
(C)	Fish	Kangaroo
(D)	Duck	Monkey

20. Refer to the given flow chart and select the correct option regarding it.

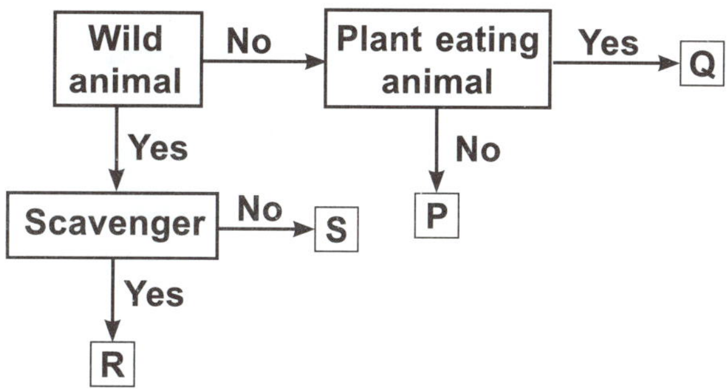

(A) P can be deer or zebra.
(B) Q can be the animal whose young one is called calf and it gives us milk.
(C) R can be vulture while S can be hyena.
(D) All of these

Darken your choice with HB Pencil

1.	Ⓐ Ⓑ Ⓒ Ⓓ	6.	Ⓐ Ⓑ Ⓒ Ⓓ	11.	Ⓐ Ⓑ Ⓒ Ⓓ	16.	Ⓐ Ⓑ Ⓒ Ⓓ
2.	Ⓐ Ⓑ Ⓒ Ⓓ	7.	Ⓐ Ⓑ Ⓒ Ⓓ	12.	Ⓐ Ⓑ Ⓒ Ⓓ	17.	Ⓐ Ⓑ Ⓒ Ⓓ
3.	Ⓐ Ⓑ Ⓒ Ⓓ	8.	Ⓐ Ⓑ Ⓒ Ⓓ	13.	Ⓐ Ⓑ Ⓒ Ⓓ	18.	Ⓐ Ⓑ Ⓒ Ⓓ
4.	Ⓐ Ⓑ Ⓒ Ⓓ	9.	Ⓐ Ⓑ Ⓒ Ⓓ	14.	Ⓐ Ⓑ Ⓒ Ⓓ	19.	Ⓐ Ⓑ Ⓒ Ⓓ
5.	Ⓐ Ⓑ Ⓒ Ⓓ	10.	Ⓐ Ⓑ Ⓒ Ⓓ	15.	Ⓐ Ⓑ Ⓒ Ⓓ	20.	Ⓐ Ⓑ Ⓒ Ⓓ

- Our body is a living machine. It has two types of organs: external organs and internal organs.
- The parts of our body that we can see are called external organs like head, arms, legs, eyes, ears, nose and tongue.
- The parts that are inside the body are called internal organs like brain, heart, lungs and stomach.

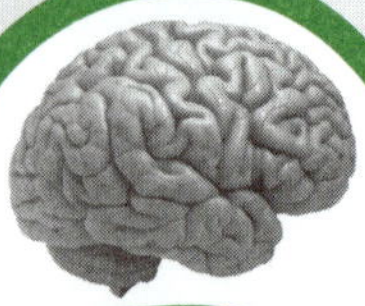

Brain helps us to think and work.

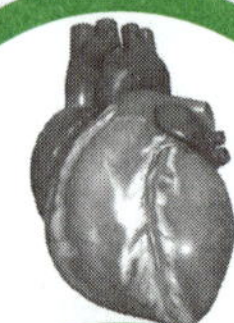

Heart pumps blood to all parts of the body.

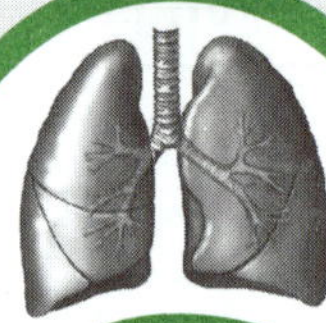

Lungs help us to breathe.

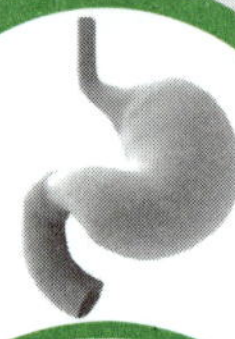

Stomach breaks down or digest the food we eat.

We have five sense organs

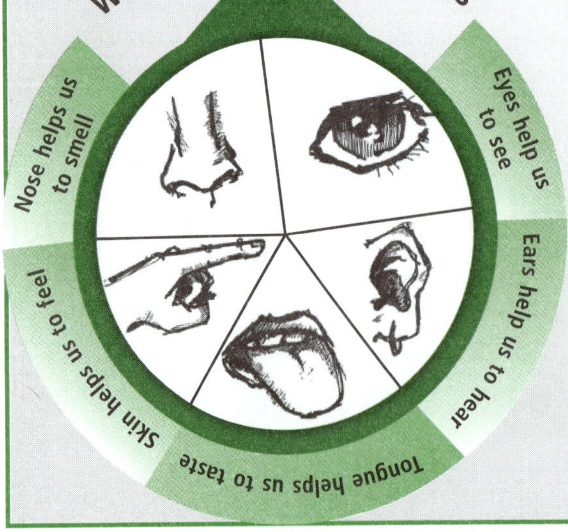

- Our body is made up of bones and muscles.
- Bones give shape and support to our body.
- Muscles help our bones to move.
- Regular exercise makes our muscles strong.
- The correct posture helps us to stay healthy and to look smart.

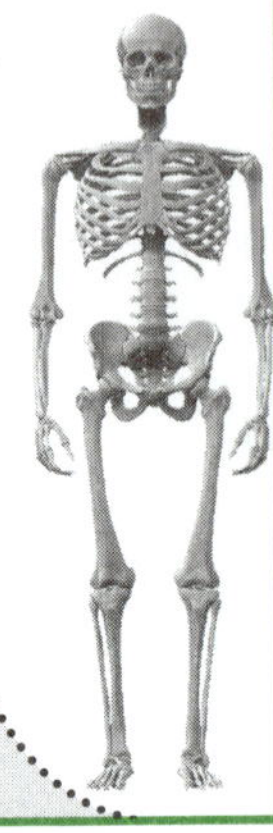

CHAPTER 3

Human Body

Test Skills

- ❑ *Our body and its parts*
- ❑ *Sense organs and our senses*
- ❑ *Importance of correct posture*
- ❑ *Bones and muscles*

1. What is the correct posture for reading?

(A) 

(B) 

(C) 

(D) All of these

2. Select the option that will complete the word in the given statement.
Our body has a framework of bones called S____E____E____O____ for support.

(A) W, D, N, L
(B) O, P, L, M
(C) K, L, T, N
(D) K, L, E, N

3. Select the INCORRECT statement from the following.

(A) There are more than 200 bones in our body.
(B) Muscles help us in movement.
(C) There are more than 600 muscles in our body.
(D) The place where two or more muscles join together is called joint.

4. 

I love shining raindrops on leaves.

Meeta

Refer to what Meeta is saying. Which sense organ has she used for that?

(A) 

(B) 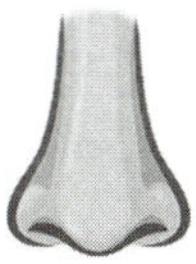

(C) 

(D) 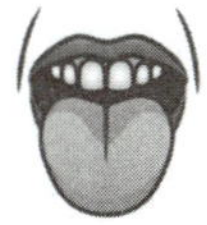

5. **Raman has difficulty in breathing. He may have some problem with his______.**

(A) Lungs (B) Stomach (C) Liver (D) Kidney

6. **I am a soft organ inside your chest. If I stop working other parts of your body will not get blood. Who am I?**

(A) 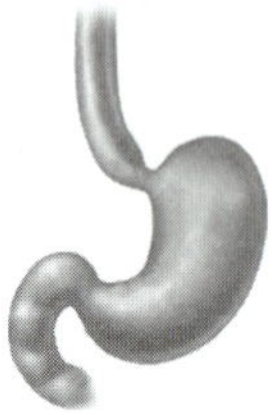

(B) 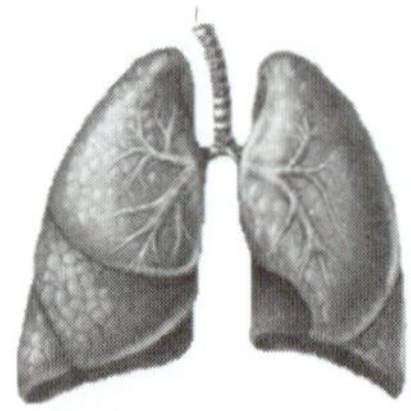

(C) 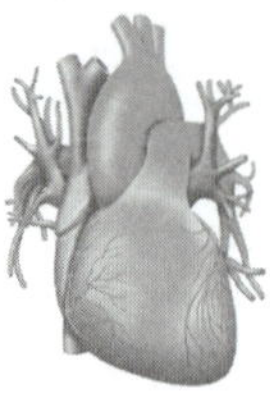

(D) None of these

7. **_________ is an activity that helps us to develop strong muscles.**

(A) Rope skipping (B) Painting (C) Jogging (D) Both (A) and (C)

8. **In which of the following activities bones and muscles are being used the least?**

(A)  (B)  (C)  (D) 

9. **Unscramble the given names of the bones and select the correct match of the bone with its function.**

	Bone	Function		Bone	Function
(A)	LUKLS	Encloses heart	(B)	SIBR	Enclose lungs
(C)	KEEN	Encloses leg	(D)	NICH	Encloses brain

10. **Match the given eatables with their supposed tastes.**

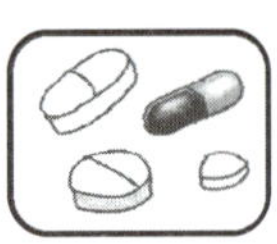   

(a) **(b)** **(c)** **(d)**

(A) (a)-Salty,(b)-Sweet, (c)-Sour, (d)-Bitter
(B) (a)-Sweet, (b)-Sour, (c)-Salty, (d)-Bitter
(C) (a)-Sour, (b)-Bitter, (c)-Salty, (d)-Sweet
(D) (a)-Bitter, (b)-Sour, (c)-Sweet, (d)-Salty

11. **Which of the following correctly shows the path that air takes in our body as we breathe in?**

(A) Nose → Gullet → Lungs
(B) Mouth → Gullet → Heart
(C) Nose → Windpipe → Lungs
(D) Lungs → Windpipe → Nose

12. **Select the correct match of activity and the muscle it makes strong.**

(A) Jogging – Arm muscles
(B) Rope skipping – Leg muscles
(C) Playing badminton – Stomach muscles
(D) Running – Neck muscles

13. **Neetu ran into the kitchen from drawing room to switch off gas stove because rice kept on it was burning. Unscramble the given letter groups to select the sense organ that she has used here.**

(A) ARES
(B) YSEE
(C) ESON
(D) KSIN

14. **Match column I with column II and select the correct option.**

Column I	Column II
(a) 	1. Swimming
(b) 	2. Playing hockey
(c) 	3. Weight lifting
(d) 	4. Cycling

(A) (a)-3, (b)-2, (c)-1, (d)-4
(B) (a)-2, (b)-1, (c)-4, (d)-3
(C) (a)-3, (b)-4, (c)-1, (d)-2
(D) (a)-2, (b)-4, (c)-1, (d)-3

15. **Hot, Cold, Soft, Smooth, Rough, Hard**

The above words are associated with which of the given sense organs?

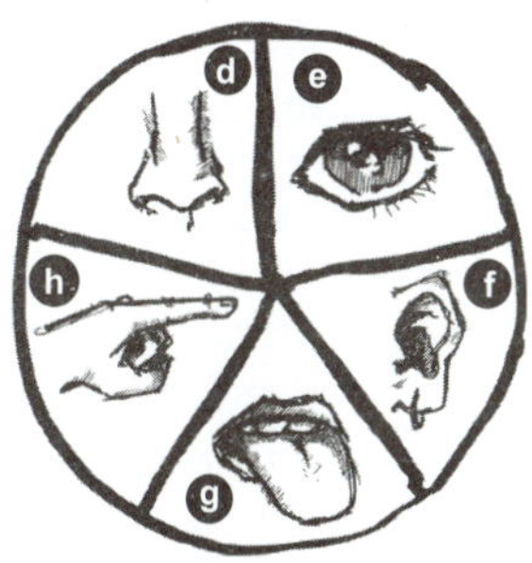

(A) d and e only
(B) e and g only
(C) h only
(D) h, e and f only

Achievers Section (HOTS)

16. Aman is blind-folded and he is asked to differentiate some pairs of items. Which of the following pairs of items can he differentiate?

Aman

(a) A glass of orange juice and a glass of plain water.
(b) A piece of red and a piece of blue cloth.
(c) A round ball and a rectangular box.
(d) An empty piggy bank and a piggy bank with some coins in it.

(A) (a) and (d) only (B) (b) and (c) only
(C) (a), (c) and (d) only (D) (a), (b), (c) and (d)

17. Read the given conversation of Ms Zarrin's pupils.

Garima	**:**	**Priya, your hair is so silky!**
Priya	**:**	**Garima! I like the fragrance of your perfume.**
Beena	**:**	**Why both of you making noise?**
Latika	**:**	**Let them talk, we will watch this video.**

Sense used by which pupil will also help her in differentiating hot coffee and cold drink?

(A) Beena (B) Garima (C) Latika (D) Priya

18. Which of the following will NOT be sensed by the respective student?

(A) 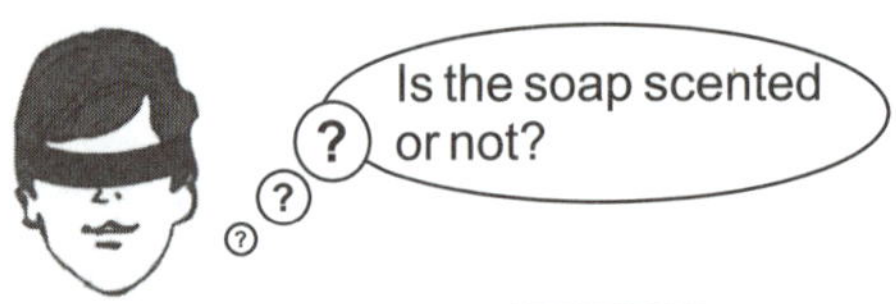

(B) 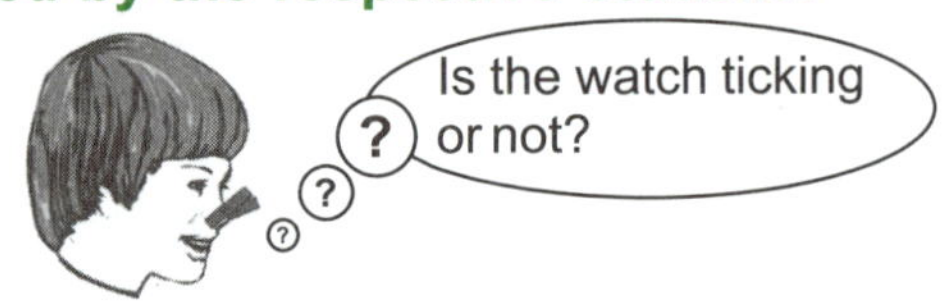

(C) 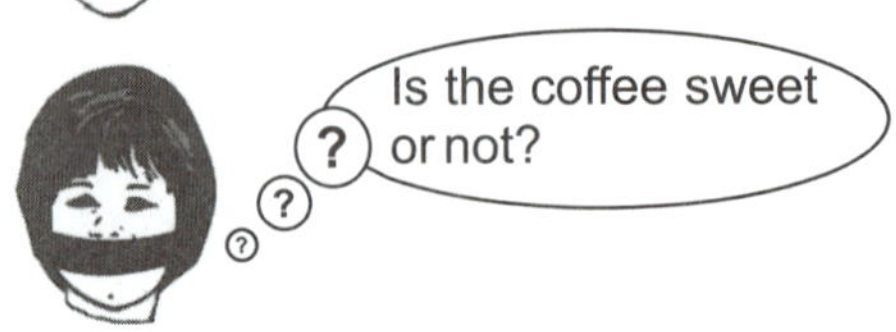

(D) 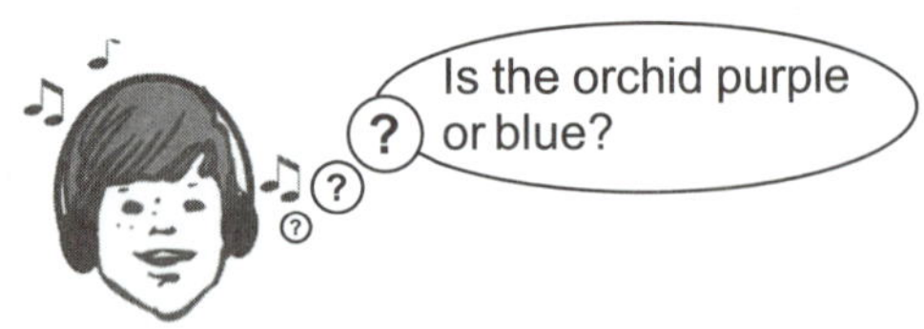

19. Refer to the given flow chart and select the INCORRECT option.

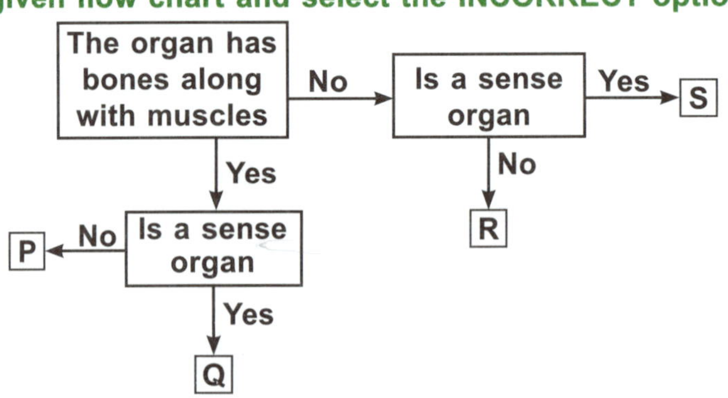

(A) Q can be the organ of hearing.
(B) P can be the organ that helps us to write.
(C) S can be the organ that pumps blood in our body.
(D) R can be the organ for digestion.

20. **Refer to the given word grid. How many sense organs (X), and internal organs (Y) are hidden in it?**

G	E	H	K	M
L	Y	E	B	S
U	E	A	T	X
N	P	R	A	A
G	R	T	I	L

	X	Y
(A)	1	4
(B)	2	2
(C)	3	2
(D)	2	1

Darken your choice with HB Pencil

1.	Ⓐ Ⓑ Ⓒ Ⓓ	6.	Ⓐ Ⓑ Ⓒ Ⓓ	11.	Ⓐ Ⓑ Ⓒ Ⓓ	16.	Ⓐ Ⓑ Ⓒ Ⓓ
2.	Ⓐ Ⓑ Ⓒ Ⓓ	7.	Ⓐ Ⓑ Ⓒ Ⓓ	12.	Ⓐ Ⓑ Ⓒ Ⓓ	17.	Ⓐ Ⓑ Ⓒ Ⓓ
3.	Ⓐ Ⓑ Ⓒ Ⓓ	8.	Ⓐ Ⓑ Ⓒ Ⓓ	13.	Ⓐ Ⓑ Ⓒ Ⓓ	18.	Ⓐ Ⓑ Ⓒ Ⓓ
4.	Ⓐ Ⓑ Ⓒ Ⓓ	9.	Ⓐ Ⓑ Ⓒ Ⓓ	14.	Ⓐ Ⓑ Ⓒ Ⓓ	19.	Ⓐ Ⓑ Ⓒ Ⓓ
5.	Ⓐ Ⓑ Ⓒ Ⓓ	10.	Ⓐ Ⓑ Ⓒ Ⓓ	15.	Ⓐ Ⓑ Ⓒ Ⓓ	20.	Ⓐ Ⓑ Ⓒ Ⓓ

Food helps us to stay alive, grow and be healthy. We get food from plants (*e.g.*, rice, wheat, etc.) and animals (*e.g.*, milk, meat, eggs, etc.). Individuals who eat meat, egg, etc. are called non-vegetarians and those who do not eat them are called vegetarians. The food we eat can be put into different groups.

Group 1 : Energy-giving foods

- These foods give you energy.
- You need energy to work and play.
- Examples are bread, chapati, sugar, jaggery, cooking oil, rice, potatoes, butter, etc.

Group 2 : Body-building foods

- These foods help you to grow.
- They help to build your bones and muscles.
- Examples are milk, nuts, peas, eggs, fish, cheese, pulses, chicken, etc.

Group 3 : Protective foods

- These foods help you to stay healthy.
- They keep diseases away.
- Examples are fresh fruits and vegetables.

Eating habits :

Do's

- Eat meals at the proper time.
- Eat clean and fresh food in a clean plate.
- Wash your hands before and after eating.
- Rinse your mouth after eating.
- Chew your food well with your mouth closed.
- Eat a healthy meal.

Don'ts

- Eat too much or too little food.
- Eat with dirty hands.
- Eat dirty and stale food.
- Always eat junk food.
- Eat while reading a book or watching T.V.

- Balanced diet is a diet that contains all the types of food in a right amount.
- We should have our meals at a fixed time everyday.
- We have **breakfast** in the morning, **lunch** in the afternoon, **snacks** in the evening and **dinner** at night.
- Sometimes, we store food for longer time using special techniques. This is called food preservation, e.g., pickling, drying, etc.

CHAPTER 4

Food

Test Skills

- ❑ ***Food sources : Plants and animals***
- ❑ ***Kinds of food such as energy giving, body building and protective foods***
- ❑ ***Balanced diet***
- ❑ ***Preservation of food***
- ❑ ***Healthy eating habits***

1. Which of these is commonly used in India for making beverages?

(A) 
Mango

(B) 
Lemon

(C) 
Coffee beans

(D) All of these

2. Which of the following we should avoid?

(A) 

(B) 

(C) 

(D) 

3. **You must brush your teeth__________a day and should visit your dentist _________ a year.**

(A) Twice, Once
(B) Twice, Twice
(C) Once, Once
(D) Thrice, Twice

4. **Select the odd one out.**

(A) Egg
(B) Fish
(C) Milk
(D) Bread

5. **__________ should be the heaviest and __________should be the lightest meal of the day.**

(A) Breakfast, Lunch
(B) Lunch, Dinner
(C) Evening snacks, Breakfast
(D) Breakfast, Dinner

6. **Select the food item that is good for our health.**

(A) 
Potato chips

(B) 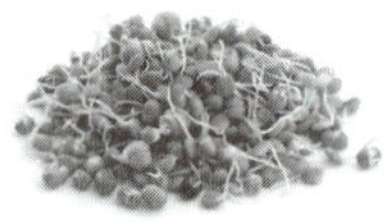
Sprouts

(C) 
French fries

(D) 
Burger

7. **The items shown in the box are__________.**

(A) Energy giving food
(B) Body building food
(C) Protective food
(D) All of these

8. **_____________ is a food preservation technique in which excess of salt and oil is added in food unlike __________ where excess of sugar is added.**

(A) Pickling, Canning
(B) Pickling, Jellying
(C) Drying, Freezing
(D) Freezing, Pickling

9. **Which of these is taken in least amount in a healthy, balanced diet?**

(A) Sugar, butter and oil
(B) Fruits and vegetables
(C) Cereal, gram and pulses
(D) Egg, milk and yoghurt

10. Misha dislikes milk and milk products and refuses to take them. In her diet, major portion is of rice, pulses and fish. This dietary routine will eventually result in weak _______.

(A) Muscles (B) Bones
(C) Teeth (D) Both (B) and (C)

11. Select the INCORRECT option.

	Do's	Don'ts
(A)	Drink water after proper purification	Eat uncovered food
(B)	Wash hands before and after meals	Talk while eating
(C)	Eat junk foods	Eat food at regular intervals everyday
(D)	Chew food properly	Eat food from roadside vendor

12. Match column I with column II and select the correct option.

Column I	Column II
(a) Dry fruit	**1. Green gram**
(b) Pulses	**2. Raisin**
(c) Beverage	**3. Coffee**
(d) Spice	**4. Coriander**
	5. Tea
	6. Almond

(A) (a)-6; (b)-1,2; (c)-3,4; (d)-5
(B) (a)-5,4; (b)-3,2; (c)-1; (d)-6
(C) (a)-2,6; (b)-1; (c)-3,5; (d)-4
(D) (a)-6; (b)-2,3; (c)-1; (d)-5,4

13. Select the INCORRECT option out of the following.

(A) Eating food in a hurry will slow down digestion.
(B) Fruits and vegetables should be washed before cutting them to keep the nutrients intact.
(C) A small baby of upto six months age is given only milk because he cannot chew and digest hard food and milk is a complete food.
(D) Soybean and jaggery are body building foods whereas cheese and vegetables are protective foods.

14. We should not skip 'X' meal because body requires it the most after hours of gap between meals. What is 'X'?

(A) Evening snacks (B) Dinner
(C) Lunch (D) Breakfast

15. 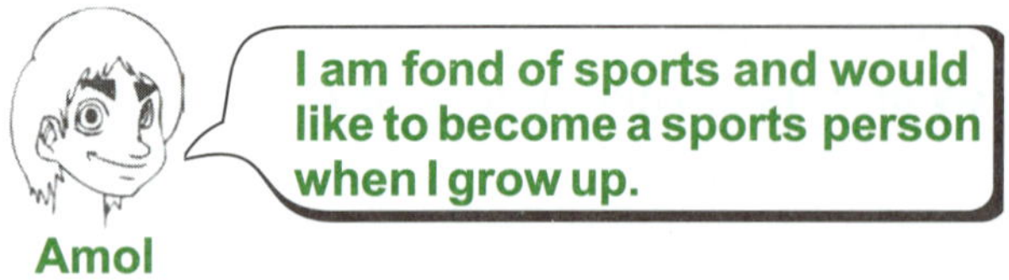

What should Amol include in his diet to develop strong muscles required for being a sportsperson?

(A) Fish, sweets and butter
(B) Fish, eggs and pulses
(C) Chips, fruits and oil
(D) Rice, jaggery and burger

Achievers Section (HOTS)

16. **Study the given flow chart and select the correct option which can fill empty spaces d, e and f.**

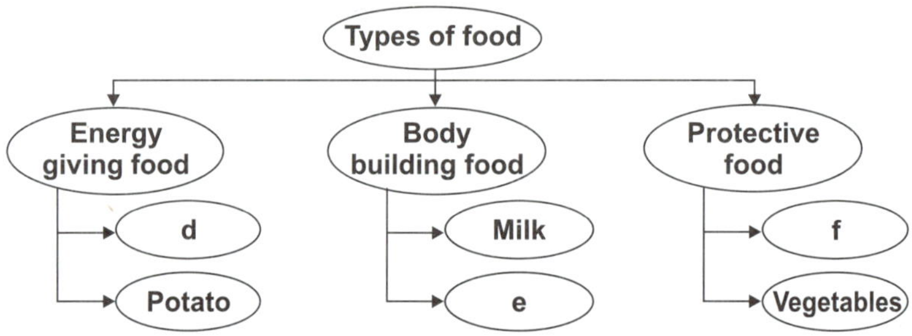

(A) d-Egg, e-Fish, f-Soybean
(B) d-Rice, e-Egg, f-Nuts
(C) d-Bread, e-Fruits, f-Cheese
(D) d-Jaggery, e-Butter, f-Fruits

17. **Why fish is kept in ice as shown in the given figure?**

(A) Fish frozen in ice is easily digestible.
(B) Fish frozen in ice can stay unspoiled for a long time.
(C) Frozen fish is more tastier.
(D) Nutrient values are lost in frozen fish.

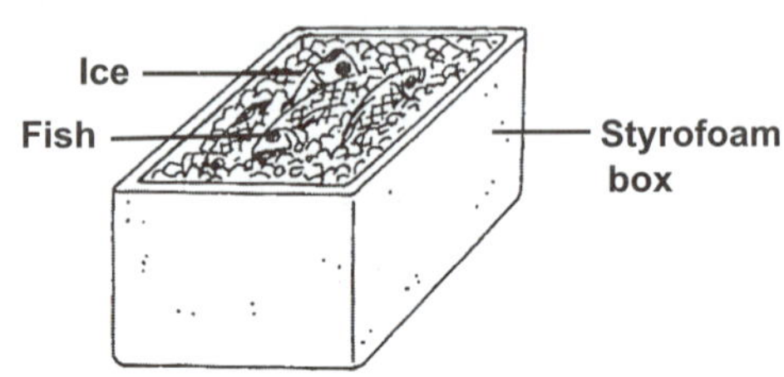

18. **Refer to the food items given in the box.**

P : Which among these will give you the most energy?
Q : Which among these is body building food?

(A) P-4, Q-1 (B) P-1, Q-3 (C) P-2, Q-3 (D) P-3, Q-2

19. Refer to the given flow chart and select the INCORRECT option regarding it.

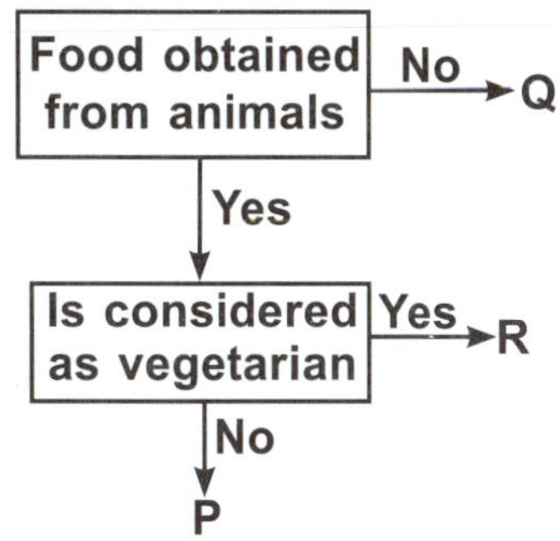

(A) There is no such food item as R.
(B) Q can be a white coloured energy giving food which is staple food of West Bengal.
(C) P can be any of the egg, meat or chicken.
(D) None of these

20. Which of the following food preservation techniques is hidden in the given word grid?

J	F	E	P
L	R	D	I
J	E	R	C
A	E	Y	K
M	Z	I	E
M	I	N	E
I	N	L	L
N	G	Y	I

(A) One that includes keeping the food in an airtight container
(B) One that includes removing all the moisture from food
(C) One that involves adding excess salt and oil
(D) One that involves keeping food at low temperatures

☺☺☺

Darken your choice with HB Pencil

1.	Ⓐ Ⓑ Ⓒ Ⓓ	6.	Ⓐ Ⓑ Ⓒ Ⓓ	11.	Ⓐ Ⓑ Ⓒ Ⓓ	16.	Ⓐ Ⓑ Ⓒ Ⓓ
2.	Ⓐ Ⓑ Ⓒ Ⓓ	7.	Ⓐ Ⓑ Ⓒ Ⓓ	12.	Ⓐ Ⓑ Ⓒ Ⓓ	17.	Ⓐ Ⓑ Ⓒ Ⓓ
3.	Ⓐ Ⓑ Ⓒ Ⓓ	8.	Ⓐ Ⓑ Ⓒ Ⓓ	13.	Ⓐ Ⓑ Ⓒ Ⓓ	18.	Ⓐ Ⓑ Ⓒ Ⓓ
4.	Ⓐ Ⓑ Ⓒ Ⓓ	9.	Ⓐ Ⓑ Ⓒ Ⓓ	14.	Ⓐ Ⓑ Ⓒ Ⓓ	19.	Ⓐ Ⓑ Ⓒ Ⓓ
5.	Ⓐ Ⓑ Ⓒ Ⓓ	10.	Ⓐ Ⓑ Ⓒ Ⓓ	15.	Ⓐ Ⓑ Ⓒ Ⓓ	20.	Ⓐ Ⓑ Ⓒ Ⓓ

A house is a place where we live and feel safe. A house protects us from the Sun, the rain and the wind. We make houses to suit our needs.

Most people live in one place for a long time. They live in permanent houses. Some people keep moving from one place to another. They live in temporary houses. The most common temporary house is caravan.

Houses are made of different materials like straw, mud, dry leaves, bamboo, wood, bricks, cement, tiles and stones. *Pucca* houses are made of bricks and cement. *Kutcha* house is made of straw, mud, dry leaves, etc.

Roofs of houses can be flat or sloping. In places which have heavy rainfall, people make houses with sloping roofs. A house may have different rooms for different purposes like kitchen for cooking, bedroom for sleeping etc.

Permanent House

Temporary House

- Clothes protect us from heat, cold, rain and wind.
- Clothes are made of fabric that is made from fibres like cotton, wool, etc.

We need warm clothes in winter. Woollen clothes keep us warm.

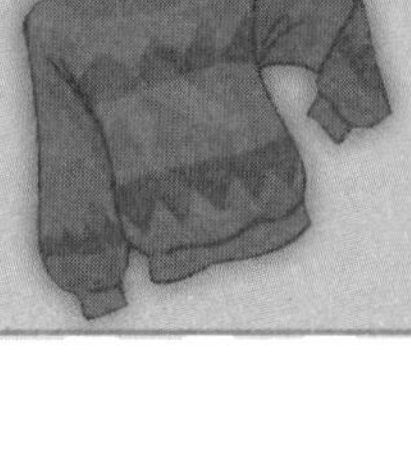

We wear cotton clothes in summer. Cotton is light and saves us from the heat.

CHAPTER 5

Housing and Clothing

Test Skills

- ❑ *Kinds of house*
- ❑ *Materials used to make houses*
- ❑ *Fibres from which clothes are made*
- ❑ *Different rooms in the house*
- ❑ *Clothes of different types*

1. Look at the picture carefully and choose the correct option.

(A) There are many homes in one building.
(B) Each home is called a flat.
(C) These houses are very strong and are made from bricks, cement and steel.
(D) All of these

2. We get __________ fibre from the animal shown here.

(A) Woollen
(B) Cotton
(C) Silk
(D) Nylon

3. In hilly areas, houses are made with sloping roofs because it prevents ________.

(A) Mountain animals from getting into house
(B) Flood water to enter into house
(C) The house from breaking down in storms
(D) Snow from collecting on the roof

4. The house shown in the given figure is called a/an ________.

(A) Caravan
(B) Igloo
(C) Stilt house
(D) Tent

5. **'Banjara' is an Indian community in which people keep moving from one place to other. Such people are called nomads. They live in ___________.**

(A)  (B) 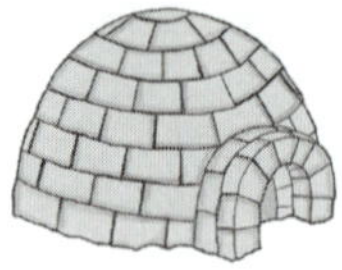 (C)  (D) 

6. **Select the clothing item that is made from the fibre whose name will be obtained by unscrambling the letters given in the box.**

I L S K

(A)  (B)  (C)  (D) 

7. **"Oh, Mom! I do not want to go to school today. Let me sleep more", said Kunal.**

In which of the following rooms Kunal should be present at this time?

(A) Bedroom
(B) Drawing room
(C) Bathroom
(D) Study room

8. **The house shown in the picture is usually built in a place where_______.**

(A) It rains a lot
(B) Wind blows very fast
(C) Heat of the Sun is extreme
(D) None of these

9. **Names of four types of house are hidden in the given puzzle. Solve the puzzle and select the house whose name is NOT hidden in the puzzle.**

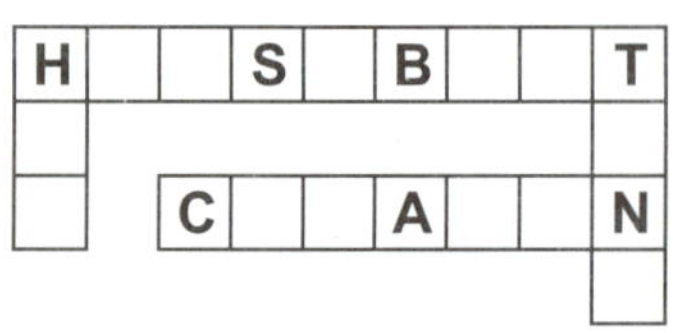

(A)  (B)  (C)  (D) 

10. **Sheena's grandmother is making cloth from wool yarn as shown in the picture. What is this method called?**

(A) Weaving
(B) Spinning
(C) Knitting
(D) None of these

11. **Ashok's house is built on wooden logs and it has sloping roofs. Ashok most probably be residing in a place where ________.**

1. Flood is common	**2. Heavy rainfall occurs**
3. Snowfall occurs	**4. Earthquakes are common**
(A) 1 and 4	(B) 1, 2 and 3
(C) 2 and 3	(D) 3 and 4

12. **Refer to the given diagram and select the correct option regarding X and Y.**

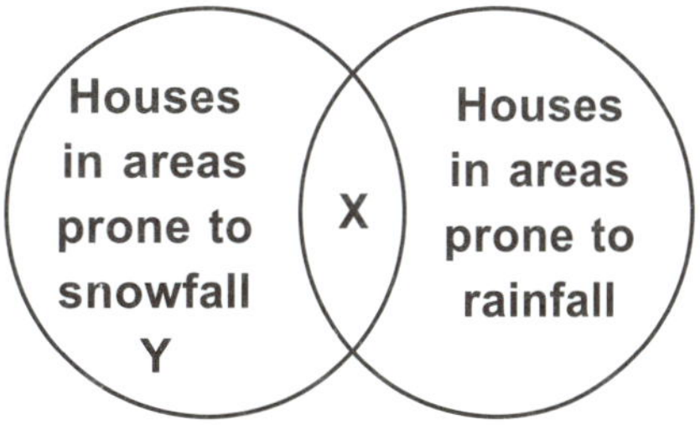

	X	Y
(A)	Sloping roof	Made of wood
(B)	Flat roof	Made on stilts
(C)	Made of ice	Flat roof
(D)	Made of mud and straw	Sloping roof

13. **The things shown in the box X can be found in which of the following rooms? [You will get the name of the rooms by cutting every third letter.]**

Box X

(A) KIGTCEHEON
(B) BARTHOROOOM
(C) BEODRMOOEM
(D) LIJVIONGRROSOM

14. **Select the INCORRECT option out of the following.**

(A) Gypsies live in temporary houses like a bungalow.
(B) A stilt house can never be found in hilly areas with snowfall.
(C) Sloping roofs are found in all permanent houses because they are cheaper to be built.
(D) All of these

15. **A material X is obtained from the given plant. The cloth made from X is not suitable to be worn in which Indian season?**

(A) Spring season
(B) Winter season
(C) Summer season
(D) Autumn season

Achievers Section (HOTS)

16. **Study the given flow chart. Which out of d, e, f, g or h best represent caravan and igloo respectively?**

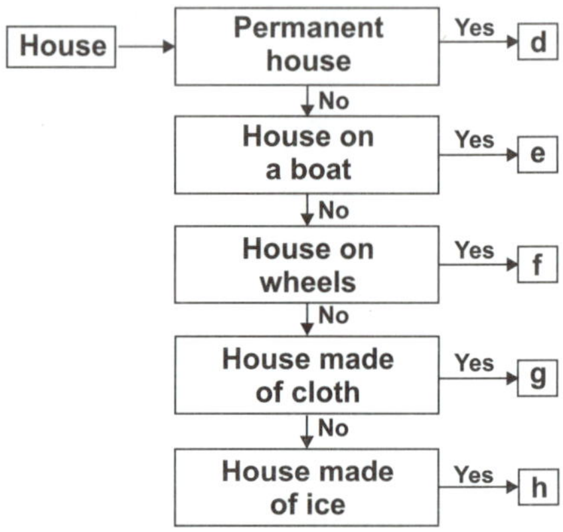

	Caravan	Igloo
(A)	e	d
(B)	f	h
(C)	f	e
(D)	g	h

17. **According to the weather forecast in Delhi given below, which of these one should wear or carry on 3rd July 20XX in case one goes out?**

1st July 20XX	2nd July 20XX	3rd July 20XX	4th July 20XX
Sunny	Cloudy	Rainy	Cloudy

(A) Raincoat
(B) Woollen socks
(C) Silk scarf
(D) Woollen cap

18. **Study the given classification chart. What could be d, e, f and g?**

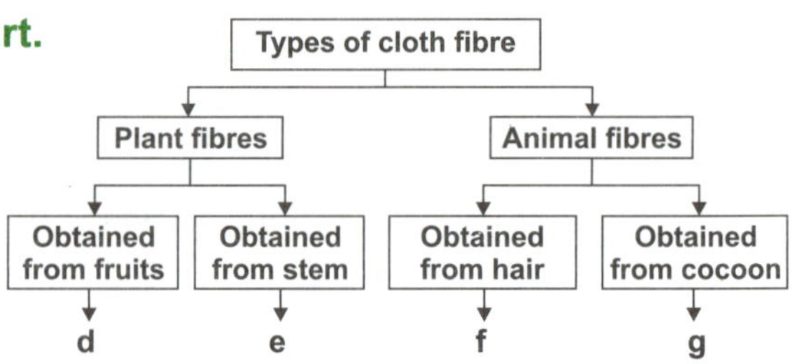

(A) d-Jute, e-Cotton, f-Wool, g-Silk
(B) d-Cotton, e-Jute, f-Wool, g-Silk
(C) d-Cotton, e-Jute, f-Silk, g-Wool
(D) d-Wool, e-Silk, f-Cotton, g-Jute

19. Namita finds a piece of cloth whose characteristics are as follows:

- **It entraps air**
- **Burns with the smell of burning hair**

This shows that the piece of cloth is made up of_______ .

(A) Synthetic fibre (B) Jute fibre

(C) Cotton fibre (D) Woollen fibre

20. Four equal sized pieces of cloth materials (P, Q, R and S), on soaking in water, absorbed water. The amount of water absorbed by them is tabulated in the given graph. Which of these is the most suitable to make a raincoat?

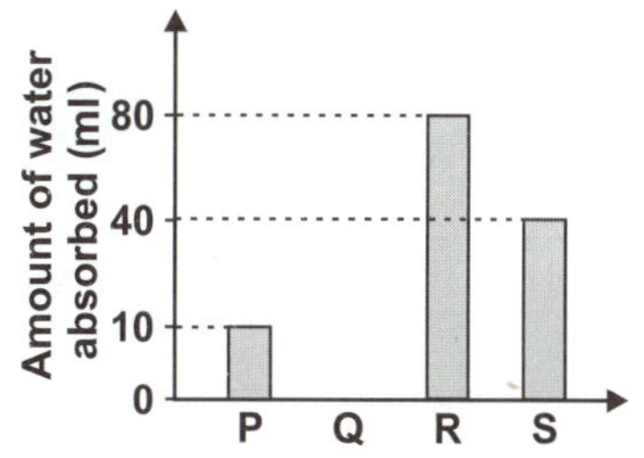

(A) R

(B) P

(C) Q

(D) S

Darken your choice with HB Pencil

1.	Ⓐ Ⓑ Ⓒ Ⓓ	6.	Ⓐ Ⓑ Ⓒ Ⓓ	11.	Ⓐ Ⓑ Ⓒ Ⓓ	16.	Ⓐ Ⓑ Ⓒ Ⓓ
2.	Ⓐ Ⓑ Ⓒ Ⓓ	7.	Ⓐ Ⓑ Ⓒ Ⓓ	12.	Ⓐ Ⓑ Ⓒ Ⓓ	17.	Ⓐ Ⓑ Ⓒ Ⓓ
3.	Ⓐ Ⓑ Ⓒ Ⓓ	8.	Ⓐ Ⓑ Ⓒ Ⓓ	13.	Ⓐ Ⓑ Ⓒ Ⓓ	18.	Ⓐ Ⓑ Ⓒ Ⓓ
4.	Ⓐ Ⓑ Ⓒ Ⓓ	9.	Ⓐ Ⓑ Ⓒ Ⓓ	14.	Ⓐ Ⓑ Ⓒ Ⓓ	19.	Ⓐ Ⓑ Ⓒ Ⓓ
5.	Ⓐ Ⓑ Ⓒ Ⓓ	10.	Ⓐ Ⓑ Ⓒ Ⓓ	15.	Ⓐ Ⓑ Ⓒ Ⓓ	20.	Ⓐ Ⓑ Ⓒ Ⓓ

CHAPTER-6 : Family and Festivals

- Members of a family have a common name. This is their surname.
- Members of a family resemble each other and may have similar habits too.
- On special occasions and festivals, we meet other members of our extended family.
- Traditions and customs are passed on from one generation to another.
- We play many indoor and outdoor games like carrom, ludo, football, etc. with family and friends.

- Celebrating festivals with our family members is a great fun.
- We all get together to celebrate the festivals.

Gurpurab

Gurpurab is celebrated by the sikhs. They celebrate Gurpurab on the birthdays and martyrs of their Gurus. They go to Gurdwaras to pray. *Langar*, a community meal is served there.

Christmas

Christmas is celebrated on 25th December every year. It is the birthday of Jesus Christ. Christmas tree is decorated with sweets and toys. The children wait for Santa Claus.

Holi

Holi is a festival of colours. People put *gulal* and throw coloured water on one another.

Diwali

Diwali is a festival of lights. People decorate their houses with oil lamps, candles or bulbs. Children enjoy fireworks and crackers. People worship Goddess Lakshmi at night.

Eid

Eid is celebrated by Muslims. They go to the Mosques to offer prayer, called *namaz*. They wish *Eid Mubarak* to all. They offer *meethi sewaian*, to guests and friends.

National Festivals

- India won freedom on 15th August 1947. **Independence Day** is celebrated on 15th August every year. The Prime Minister hoists the National Flag at the Red Fort in Delhi and gives speech.
- On 26th January 1950, our country became a republic. **Republic Day** is celebrated on 26th January every year. The armed forces, folk dancers and school children in colourful dresses take part in a parade at Rajpath in New Delhi.

Family occasions

We attend weddings in the family. We celebrate birthdays of our family members

CHAPTER 6

Family and Festivals

Test Skills

- Family and family members
- Traditions and customs of families
- Relations and responsibilities amongst family members
- Special occasions in the family
- Festivals and celebrations
- National festivals
- Indoor and outdoor activities

1. **Which option shows all the indoor activities?**
   (A) Ludo, Carrom, Cycling
   (B) Chess, Table tennis, Cricket
   (C) Football, Watching television, Dancing
   (D) Carrom, Chess, Table tennis

2. **The given picture shows which occasion in the family ?**

   (A) Birthday celebration
   (B) Anniversary
   (C) Wedding
   (D) Housewarming party

3. **My friend Ravi Gupta's mother calls him 'Guddu' lovingly. Gupta is his __________ name and Guddu is his __________ name.**
   (A) Middle, Nick (B) Nick, Middle (C) Sur, Nick (D) Sur, Middle

4. **What is the name of the Samadhi of our Rashtrapita?**
   (A) Raj Ghat (B) Vijay Ghat (C) Shaheed Sthal (D) Shakti Sthal

5. **Ali is very happy today. He is wearing new clothes and is enjoying *meethi sewaian* made by his mother. Today is __________.**
   (A) Christmas (B) Eid (C) Holi (D) Diwali

6. **Priya is married to Vishal. Vishal is __________ of Priya.**
   (A) Fiance (B) Husband (C) Brother (D) Father

7. **Select the odd one out among the following.**
   (A) Ludo (B) Carrom (C) Chess (D) Football

8. **Hindus greet each other with the folded hands gesture as shown below. What holds true regarding this greeting?**

   1. **It means *namaste* which means "I bow to you".**
   2. **It expresses deep respect.**
   3. **It expresses deep sorrow.**
   4. **It means *namaste* which literally means 'happy journey'.**

   (A) 1 and 2 only (B) 1 and 3 only (C) 3 and 4 only (D) 2 and 4 only

9. **Which of the following are benefits of outdoor activities?**
   1. **They help in bonding with people.**
   2. **They give physical benefits and help in improving health.**
   3. **They increase stress and challenges of life.**
   4. **They increase awareness and concern about our duties to develop a healthy environment.**

   (A) 1, 2 and 4 only (B) 2 and 3 only
   (C) 1 and 3 only (D) 1, 2, 3 and 4

10. **Which of these shows your contribution as a helping hand in your family?**

   (A)  (B)  (C)  (D) All of these

11. **Match the column I with column II and select the correct option.**

	Column I		Column II
(a)	S. Radhakrishnan	1.	Children's Day
(b)	S. Ramanujan	2.	National Unity Day
(c)	J. L. Nehru	3.	Mathematics Day
(d)	Sardar Patel	4.	Teacher's Day

   (A) (a)-2, (b)-3, (c)-4, (d)-1 (B) (a)-1, (b)-4, (c)-3, (d)-2
   (C) (a)-4, (b)-1, (c)-3, (d)-2 (D) (a)-4, (b)-3, (c)-1, (d)-2

12. **Mr X wears turban and is a follower of Guru Gobind Singh. He goes to a __________ to offer prayers.**

   (A)  (B)  (C)  (D) 

13. **Rohan made four groups each with two activities of similar kind, but he made one mistake while pairing activities in one of the groups. Select the INCORRECT group.**

(A) Ludo and Carrom
(B) Table tennis and Polo
(C) Billiards and Chess
(D) Cricket and Football

14. **Refer to the given conversation between four friends and find out the friend who is correct.**

(A) 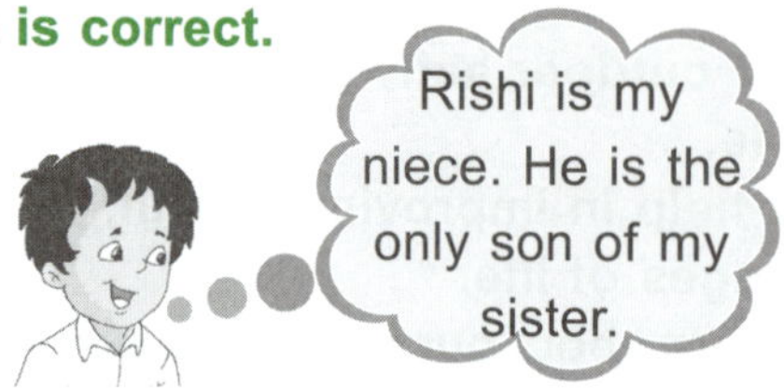

Ajay

(B) 

Sumit

(C) 

Ananya

(D) 

Rati

15. **Identify the festival being celebrated as shown in the given picture and tell how people celebrate this festival.**

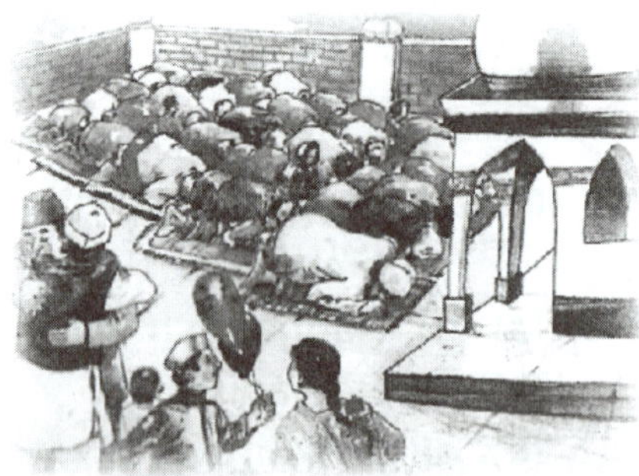

(A) They decorate trees with sweets and toys.
(B) They go to the mosques to offer prayers and eat *meethi sewaian*.
(C) They serve *langar* in the community.
(D) They throw coloured water on one another.

Achievers Section (HOTS)

16. **The effigies of two persons are burnt every year along with Ravana on Dussehra. Who are those two persons and what are their relations with Ravana ?**

(A) Kumbhkaran - brother, Meghnath - son
(B) Meghnath - brother, Kumbhkaran - son
(C) Vibhishan and Kumbhkaran - both brothers
(D) Kumbhkaran and Meghnath - both brothers

17. **Megha and Harsha are non-siblings who have common great grandparents but not common grandparents. They are _______ .**

(A) First cousins
(B) Second cousins
(C) Step-cousins
(D) None of these

18.

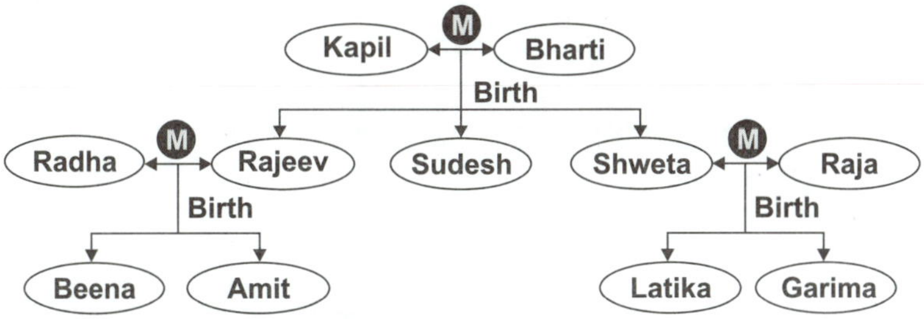

M : Stands for Marriage

Study the above family tree and select the correct option regarding it.

(A) Rajeev and Sudesh are cousins.
(B) Garima is Sudesh's aunty.
(C) Latika is Rajeev's niece.
(D) Amit is Kapil's son-in-law.

19. Study the given family tree of Shalini. Select the correct option regarding it.

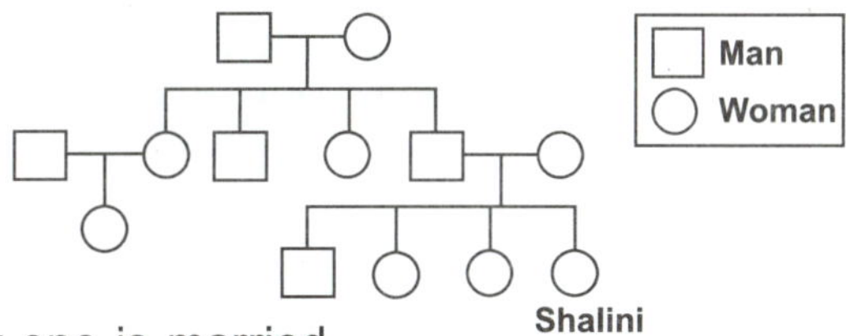

(A) Shalini has two cousins.
(B) Shalini has two elder brothers and one younger sister.
(C) Among the two aunts of Shalini, only one is married.
(D) Shalini's grandfather has three daughters and one son.

20. Refer to the given word chop table and find out the boxes which give :
a. Name of the festival that marks birthday of Jesus Christ.
b. Name of the festival of colours.

1 CUER	2 HO	3 ID	4 UDW
5 DI	6 WA	7 STM	8 ARA
9 CHRI	10 AS	11 EI	12 LI

	a	b
(A)	1, 4, 7	5, 6, 12
(B)	9, 7, 10	2, 12
(C)	6, 11	9, 7
(D)	2, 3, 5	7, 8

☺☺☺

Darken your choice with HB Pencil

1.	Ⓐ Ⓑ Ⓒ Ⓓ	6.	Ⓐ Ⓑ Ⓒ Ⓓ	11.	Ⓐ Ⓑ Ⓒ Ⓓ	16.	Ⓐ Ⓑ Ⓒ Ⓓ
2.	Ⓐ Ⓑ Ⓒ Ⓓ	7.	Ⓐ Ⓑ Ⓒ Ⓓ	12.	Ⓐ Ⓑ Ⓒ Ⓓ	17.	Ⓐ Ⓑ Ⓒ Ⓓ
3.	Ⓐ Ⓑ Ⓒ Ⓓ	8.	Ⓐ Ⓑ Ⓒ Ⓓ	13.	Ⓐ Ⓑ Ⓒ Ⓓ	18.	Ⓐ Ⓑ Ⓒ Ⓓ
4.	Ⓐ Ⓑ Ⓒ Ⓓ	9.	Ⓐ Ⓑ Ⓒ Ⓓ	14.	Ⓐ Ⓑ Ⓒ Ⓓ	19.	Ⓐ Ⓑ Ⓒ Ⓓ
5.	Ⓐ Ⓑ Ⓒ Ⓓ	10.	Ⓐ Ⓑ Ⓒ Ⓓ	15.	Ⓐ Ⓑ Ⓒ Ⓓ	20.	Ⓐ Ⓑ Ⓒ Ⓓ

Occupation is the job that a person does. Everyone has to work to earn money. That work becomes his job. People have different occupations.

An engineer designs and repairs machines, roads, etc.

A policeman maintains law and order.

A doctor treats the patients. A doctor uses stethoscope to listen to the heartbeat of patients.

A nurse takes care of the sick people.

A banker is the one who conducts the business of banking.

A farmer grows crops, fruits and vegetables for us. Some tools used by a farmer are khurpi, plough, sickle and tractor.

A postman brings letters and parcels.

A blacksmith makes and repairs things made of iron.

A fireman puts out the fire.

A tailor stitches our clothes. The tailor uses threads, needles, scissors and sewing machine to stitch clothes.

A carpenter makes and repairs wooden things.

A grocer sells food items and other things that are used at home.

A mechanic repairs our vehicles. The tools used are screwdriver, chain tool, blowgun and sockets.

A plumber fits and repairs water pipes.

A potter makes clay pots for us.

CHAPTER 7

Occupations

Test Skills

- Professionals and their roles
- Work places
- Tools and techniques used in different occupations

1. **Who is a carpenter?**
   (A) One who paints the house
   (B) One who paints the car
   (C) One who drives the car
   (D) One who makes the furniture

2. **A person who studies Earth's atmosphere and the variations in the atmospheric conditions that produce weather is called _______.**
   (A) Astronomist
   (B) Botanist
   (C) Geologist
   (D) Meteorologist

3. **The person shown in the given figure is a/an _______.**

   (A) Lawyer
   (B) Policeman
   (C) Engineer
   (D) Doctor

4. **If a tap in your house is leaking, you should call a _______ to get it fixed.**
   (A) Plumber
   (B) Architect
   (C) Mason
   (D) Cobbler

5. **(X , X ! mend my shoe. Get it done by half past two.) Who is 'X' in the given rhyme?**
   (A) Carpenter
   (B) Tailor
   (C) Potter
   (D) Cobbler

6. **Select the professional who is NOT related to the other three.**
   (A) Painter
   (B) Mason
   (C) Architect
   (D) Barber

7. **The musicians do NOT use which of the following items?**

(A)  (B) 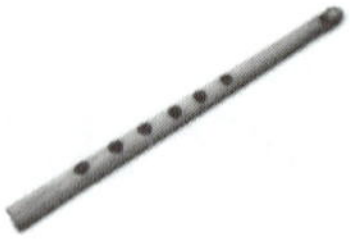 (C) 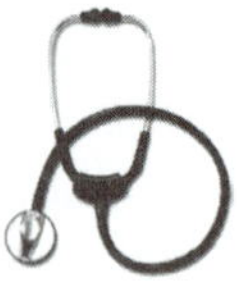 (D) 

8. **Read the statements made by four children.**
Megha : The painter paints the house.
Priya : The carpenter digs the land.
Rohan : The plumber builds the wall.
Manish : The electrician fits wires, switches and bulbs.
Which child/children made INCORRECT statement?
(A) Megha and Manish only
(B) Priya only
(C) Manish and Rohan only
(D) Priya and Rohan only

9. **Three of the following tools are used by the same professional. Select the odd one.**

(A)  (B) 

(C) 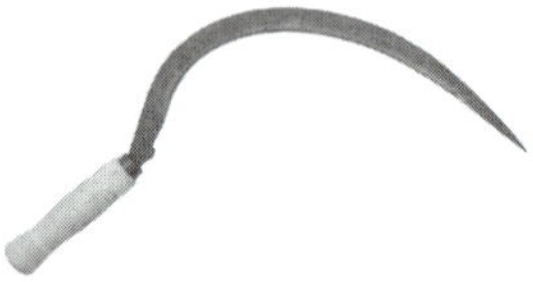 (D) 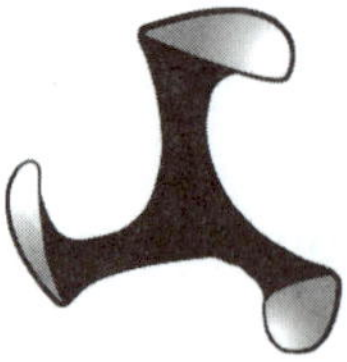

10. **Refer to the picture shown here. Raju should go to a _______.**

(A) Greengrocer
(B) Chemist
(C) Doctor
(D) Electrician

11. **Match the column I with column II and select the correct option.**

Column I | **Column II**

(a) 

1. 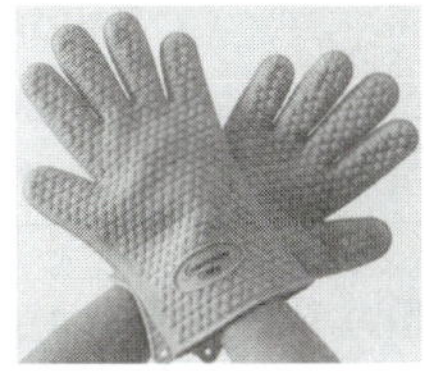

(b) 

2. 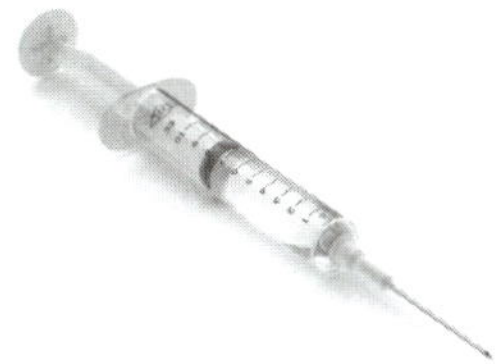

(c) 

3. 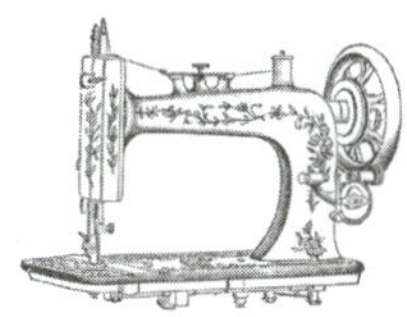

(A) (a)-2, (b)-3, (c)-1
(B) (a)-1, (b)-2, (c)-3
(C) (a)-3, (b)-2, (c)-1
(D) (a)-2, (b)-1, (c)-3

12. **Four friends P, Q, R and S made four statements. Which friend has made an INCORRECT statement?**

(A) P – Today is my brother's birthday. I am going to a baker to order a cake.
(B) Q – I want to eat chilly paneer today so, I am going to a sweeper to get some paneer.
(C) R – I have to buy some medicines prescribed by my doctor so, I am going to a chemist.
(D) S – I want to make tomato soup so, I am going to a greengrocer to buy some tomatoes.

13. **Unscramble the given letter groups and select the option that gives the name of the professional who sells notebooks, pencils, pens, etc.**

(A) AKBER (B) TSATIONRE (C) ARMFER (D) EROGCR

14. **The curries we eat in our food are cooked using vegetables sold by __X__ and spices sold by __Y__. Both vegetables and spices are grown by __Z__. Select the option that correctly fills the blanks in the above sentence.**

	X	Y	Z
(A)	Farmer	Grocer	Baker
(B)	Baker	Tailor	Cobbler
(C)	Greengrocer	Grocer	Farmer
(D)	Greengrocer	Baker	Painter

15. Which of the following services is/are done by the professional shown in the given picture?

(A) Accepting deposits from the public and keeping them safe.
(B) Sending and receiving telegrams and money orders.
(C) Giving loans to the customers and charging interest from them.
(D) Both (A) and (C)

Achievers Section (HOTS)

16. Which of the following statements is true for the place shown in the given picture?

(A) It helps us to send messages from one place to another.
(B) It has an ambulance to carry the letters.
(C) We buy inland letters and envelopes from here.
(D) Both (A) and (C)

17. Which of the following statements holds true for the professional shown in the given picture?

(A) She makes a drawing of the house before it is built.
(B) She supervises and maintains construction of the house after it is built.
(C) She designs and repairs the furniture of the house.
(D) None of these

18. Study the given flow chart showing housemakers and things with which they work. Select the correct option regarding it.

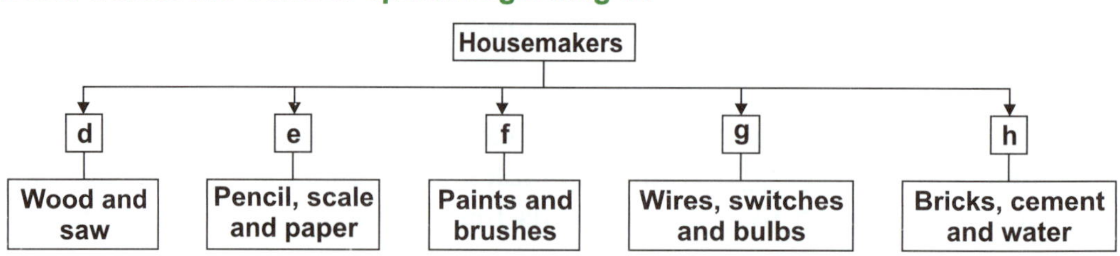

(A) d is an architect and g is an electrician.
(B) f is a painter and d is a mason.
(C) e is an architect and h is a mason.
(D) g is a carpenter and e is an electrician.

19. Select the correct match.

	Tool		Professional		Tool		Professional
(A)		—	Tailor	(B)	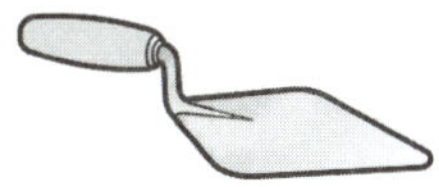	—	Mechanic
(C)		—	Cobbler	(D)	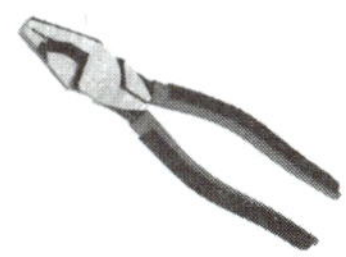	—	Farmer

20. Names of some professionals are hidden in the given word grid.

a. How many names are hidden?

b. How many of them require skills for the work and not high education?

N	T	A	F	T	S	S	N
O	A	B	A	R	B	E	R
A	I	S	R	C	H	E	H
P	L	U	M	B	E	R	N
P	O	R	E	H	G	I	A
Q	R	V	R	I	K	B	A

	a	b
(A)	Four	Two
(B)	Five	Three
(C)	Four	Four
(D)	Three	Two

☺☺☺

Darken your choice with HB Pencil

1.	Ⓐ Ⓑ Ⓒ Ⓓ	6.	Ⓐ Ⓑ Ⓒ Ⓓ	11.	Ⓐ Ⓑ Ⓒ Ⓓ	16.	Ⓐ Ⓑ Ⓒ Ⓓ
2.	Ⓐ Ⓑ Ⓒ Ⓓ	7.	Ⓐ Ⓑ Ⓒ Ⓓ	12.	Ⓐ Ⓑ Ⓒ Ⓓ	17.	Ⓐ Ⓑ Ⓒ Ⓓ
3.	Ⓐ Ⓑ Ⓒ Ⓓ	8.	Ⓐ Ⓑ Ⓒ Ⓓ	13.	Ⓐ Ⓑ Ⓒ Ⓓ	18.	Ⓐ Ⓑ Ⓒ Ⓓ
4.	Ⓐ Ⓑ Ⓒ Ⓓ	9.	Ⓐ Ⓑ Ⓒ Ⓓ	14.	Ⓐ Ⓑ Ⓒ Ⓓ	19.	Ⓐ Ⓑ Ⓒ Ⓓ
5.	Ⓐ Ⓑ Ⓒ Ⓓ	10.	Ⓐ Ⓑ Ⓒ Ⓓ	15.	Ⓐ Ⓑ Ⓒ Ⓓ	20.	Ⓐ Ⓑ Ⓒ Ⓓ

Good habits to follow

- Don't bite nails.
- Don't eat fallen food.
- Don't spit on road.
- Cover your mouth and nose while sneezing, coughing or yawning.
- Throw garbage in dustbin.
- Wash hands with soap after going to the toilet.

Ways to stay healthy

Some of our safety rules

On Road

- Always walk on footpath.
- While walking, use zebra crossing to cross the road.
- Do not run or play near the road.
- Obey the traffic lights.

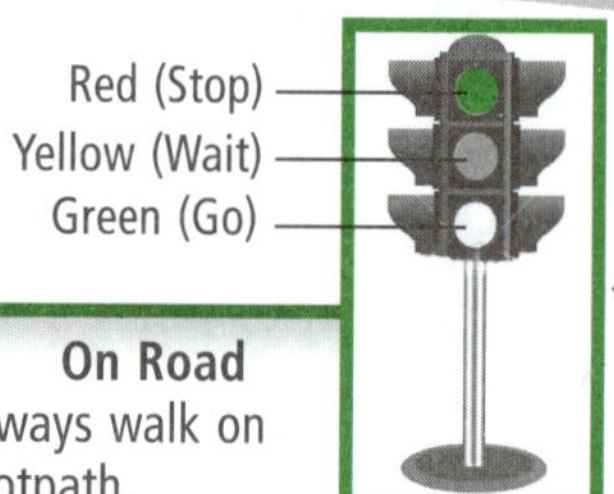

At Home

- Don't touch or play with electric wires or plug points; sharp objects like scissors, knives and blades.
- Don't play with fire.

At School

- Never run around benches and don't climb on them.
- Don't run down or up the stairs.

In Playground

- Never push your friends while playing.
- Follow the rules of games while playing.

Other safety rules

- Always swim in the presence of an adult.
- During festivals, light candles with the help of adults.
- Don't play with crackers.

If someone gets hurt give immediate help to him. This is called "First Aid".

CHAPTER 8

Good Habits and Safety Rules

Test Skills

- *Good habits to stay healthy*
- *Safety rules at home, school, playground and other places*
- *First aid*

1. __________ is the immediate help given to a person who is hurt, before the doctor comes.

(A) Critical aid
(B) First aid
(C) Medical treatment
(D) Intensive treatment

2. Which of these you should NOT do while eating?

(A) Stuff your mouth
(B) Chew with mouth closed
(C) Chew food slowly
(D) Avoid talking

3. Always walk on the __________ and cross the road at a __________ if there is one.

(A) Zebra crossing, Footpath
(B) Road, Zebra crossing
(C) Footpath, Subway
(D) Road, Footpath

4. Always take __________ with you when you go for swimming.

(A) Swimming float
(B) Swimming goggles
(C) Helmet
(D) Both (A) and (B)

5. Refer to the given picture. Is the boy following safety rules?

(A) Yes, because he is not flying kite in the ground.
(B) No, because he is not wearing float.
(C) Yes, because he is wearing a cap.
(D) No, because he is flying kite on terrace without railings.

6. **We should never play with __________.**

(A) Matchbox and matchstick
(B) Football
(C) Blade
(D) Both (A) and (C)

7. **If your friend gets hurt while playing, you should __________.**

(A) Start crying
(B) Run away
(C) Put sand on the wound
(D) Call an adult

8. **Ashok goes to school on a bicycle. Which of these safety rules should he follow?**

(A) He should keep to the right of the road.
(B) He should give signals before taking turns.
(C) He should cross the road by using zebra crossing.
(D) All of these

9. **Refer to the safety rules written on the board.**

When you swim

1. Do not play rough games in the pool.
2. Always swim in the deep end.
3. Always take a rubber tube with you.
4. Avoid swimming with a grown-up near you.

Which of the safety rules is/are INCORRECT?

(A) 1 and 3 only
(B) 4 only
(C) 2 and 4 only
(D) 1, 2 and 3 only

10. **Which of these you should avoid doing at home?**

(A) 

(B) 

(C) 

(D) All of these

11. **Which of the following is a bad habit?**

(A) 

(B) 

(C) 

(D) 

12. **Student(s) doing which one of the following activities is/are least likely to get hurt?**

(A) 

(B) 

(C) 

(D) 

13. **Rani and Adi were playing when Adi fainted. Rani should __________.**

(A) Pour hot water on Adi's head
(B) Wrap Adi in a blanket
(C) Tie bandage on Adi's head
(D) None of these

14. **Ramesh takes healthy diet daily still he falls ill frequently. What could be the reason for it?**

(A) He does not comb his hair daily.
(B) He does not trim his nails regularly.
(C) He does not wash his hands properly before eating.
(D) Both (B) and (C)

15. **It is not a good habit to ________.**

(A) Throw waste into the dustbin

(B) Put clean water for birds to drink

(C) Waste food by taking excess food than needed

(D) Keep food covered

Achievers Section (HOTS)

16. **Match the given columns and select the correct option.**

	Safety rules		**Activity**
(a)	**Keep sitting**	**(1)**	**Playing**
(b)	**Take a rubber tube**	**(2)**	**Swimming**
(c)	**Use a park or garden**	**(3)**	**Travelling**
(d)	**Use the footpath**	**(4)**	**Walking**

(A) (a)-(1), (b)-(2), (c)-(4), (d)-(3)

(B) (a)-(3), (b)-(2), (c)-(1), (d)-(4)

(C) (a)-(3), (b)-(2), (c)-(4), (d)-(1)

(D) (a)-(2), (b)-(3), (c)-(1), (d)-(4)

17. **The given things can be dangerous as they all**

(A) Have sharp edges which can cut your hands

(B) Can catch fire easily and can burn you

(C) Are chemicals and can be harmful

(D) None of these.

18.

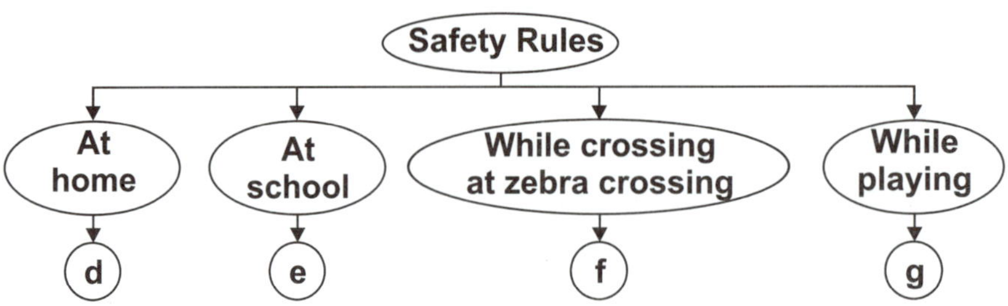

Study the above given flow chart and select the correct option regarding it.

(A) e - Do not stand in the queue

(B) d - Do not touch stoves, heaters, toasters or electric fan when they are switched on

(C) g - Do not fly kites in open fields

(D) f - Do not cross the road when the traffic light is red for vehicles

DIRECTION (Q. No. 19 and 20) : Refer to the given word grid and answer the following questions.

Z	R	F	K	S	A	H
E	O	O	N	U	C	E
B	S	O	E	B	R	L
R	S	T	E	W	O	M
S	U	B	W	A	Y	E
A	I	R	U	Z	E	T
C	N	I	A	G	B	R

19. The safety tool used in which of the following sports is NOT hidden in the given grid?

(A) Cycling

(B) Cricket

(C) Swimming

(D) Skating

20. We should cross a road using an __X__ . Find X from the grid.

(A) Subway (B) Foot bridge

(C) Zebra crossing (D) All of these

☺☺☺

Darken your choice with HB Pencil

1.	Ⓐ Ⓑ Ⓒ Ⓓ	6.	Ⓐ Ⓑ Ⓒ Ⓓ	11.	Ⓐ Ⓑ Ⓒ Ⓓ	16.	Ⓐ Ⓑ Ⓒ Ⓓ
2.	Ⓐ Ⓑ Ⓒ Ⓓ	7.	Ⓐ Ⓑ Ⓒ Ⓓ	12.	Ⓐ Ⓑ Ⓒ Ⓓ	17.	Ⓐ Ⓑ Ⓒ Ⓓ
3.	Ⓐ Ⓑ Ⓒ Ⓓ	8.	Ⓐ Ⓑ Ⓒ Ⓓ	13.	Ⓐ Ⓑ Ⓒ Ⓓ	18.	Ⓐ Ⓑ Ⓒ Ⓓ
4.	Ⓐ Ⓑ Ⓒ Ⓓ	9.	Ⓐ Ⓑ Ⓒ Ⓓ	14.	Ⓐ Ⓑ Ⓒ Ⓓ	19.	Ⓐ Ⓑ Ⓒ Ⓓ
5.	Ⓐ Ⓑ Ⓒ Ⓓ	10.	Ⓐ Ⓑ Ⓒ Ⓓ	15.	Ⓐ Ⓑ Ⓒ Ⓓ	20.	Ⓐ Ⓑ Ⓒ Ⓓ

TRANSPORT

Transport or we can say transportation, is the movement of people, animals and things from one place to another. Modes of transport or means of transport is a term used for different ways to perform transport. Each mode has its own infrastructure, vehicles and operations.

Means of transport

There are three means of transport : Land, Water and Air

Air transport

- It is the fastest means of transport.
- Aeroplanes, helicopters, jet planes, etc., are used for it.

Water transport

- Boats, ships, sailboats, steamers, submarines, etc., are used for it.
- These carry people and goods across rivers and seas.

Land transport

- Bicycle, cycle-rickshaws (run by man power); bullock carts, tongas (run by animals); car, bus, truck, etc. (run by petrol or diesel or gas engines); trains (run by steam or diesel or electric engines); etc. are used for it.

COMMUNICATION

Means of communication

Communication means to speak, write or use signs and sounds to share ideas and information with each other.

Postal communication

- Postcards, aerogrammes inland letters and letters in stamped envelope are means of postal communication.

Modern means of communication

- Telephone, mobile/cellular phone, e-mail, fax, etc. are its examples.
- These are the fastest means of communication.

Means of mass communication

- Newspapers, magazines, radio, television and internet are its examples.

- People who cannot speak or hear, communicate through sign language.

- A direction is the way in which a person or a thing moves.
- Map is a diagram or a drawing of a particular area or place on a paper.
- Road signs give information or instruction to road users.
- Road signs, maps and directions help us to locate things.

CHAPTER 9 Transport and Communication

Test Skills

- ***Means of transport***
- ***Road signs, maps and directions***
- ***Means of communication***

1. **Stand facing the rising Sun in the morning. In front of you lies the _______ and behind you is, the ________. Between them to the right side is _______ and to left side is ________.**

   (A) East, West, North, South
   (B) East, West, South, North
   (C) West, East, South, North
   (D) North, South, East, West

2. **Sonu made four groups each with two means of transport with some similarity. In doing so, he made an incorrect group. Identify the INCORRECT group.**

   (A) Helicopter, Aeroplane
   (B) Car, Submarine
   (C) Sailboat, Steamship
   (D) Truck, Bus

3. **Select the odd one out among the following.**

   (A) 
   (B) 
   (C) 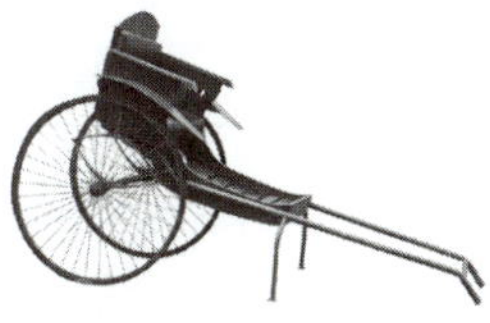
   (D) 

4. **The road sign shown here means that a/an____________ is nearby.**

   (A) Hospital
   (B) School
   (C) Bus stop
   (D) Airport

5. ____________ is a means of verbal communication.

(A) Radio (B) Television
(C) Mime (D) Both (A) and (B)

6. Using which of the given means of transport we can travel maximum distance in a minimum time?

(A) 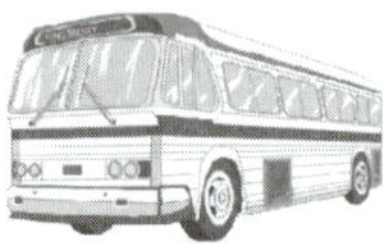 (B)  (C)  (D) 

7. Select the vehicle that is a part of the same mode of transport as shown in given picture.

(A)  (B) 

(C)  (D) 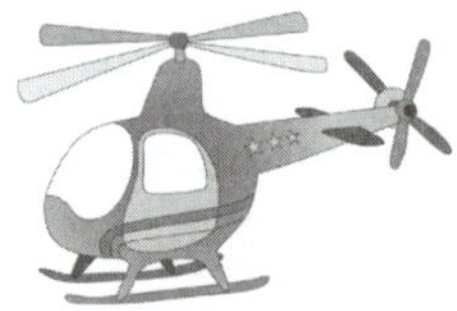

8. Refer to the given picture. Which road sign is the child ignoring while crossing the closed gate?

(A)  (B) 

(C)  (D) 

9. The traffic police officer is signalling to stop vehicles approaching from __________.

(A) Behind
(B) Front
(C) Left and right sides
(D) Both (A) and (B)

10. A word is encircled in each option which does NOT belong to the group. In which option INCORRECT word is encircled for the group?

(A) Radio, Stamps, Postcard, Letter box

(B) Newspaper, Radio, Television, Fax

(C) Letter box, Telephone, E-mail, Postcard

(D) Money order, Telegram, Television, Parcel

11. Which of the following can be run by gas engines?

a b c d e

(A) a and b
(B) b and d
(C) c and b
(D) a and e

12. Full form of PIN is __________.

(A) Postal Index Number

(B) Payable Index Number

(C) Printed Indian Newspaper

(D) Permanent Index Number

13. Which of the following is INCORRECT regarding roadways?

(A) Roads connect different cities.
(B) It is the costliest mode of transportation.
(C) It has various types of road sign.
(D) It is through roads that we reach railway stations, airports and seaports.

14. Now-a-days, people sitting at far off places can talk to and see each other and express their views with the help of telecommunication and computer. This is done through ______.

(A) E-mail
(B) Video conferencing
(C) News telecast
(D) Fax

15. **Study the given map of Richa's locality. What is located to South of the temple?**

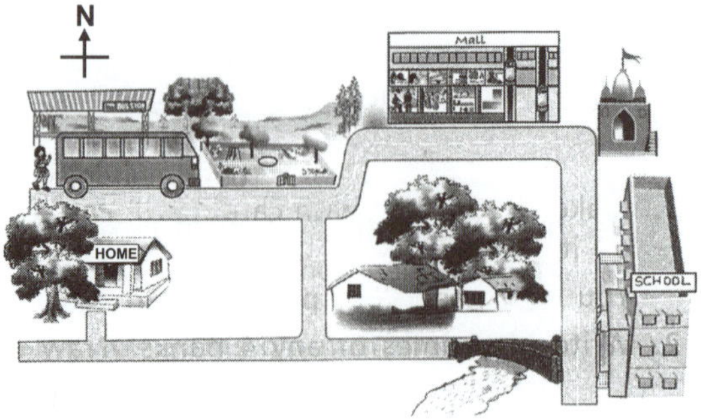

(A) Richa's home (B) Bus stop (C) Mall (D) School

Achievers Section (HOTS)

16. **Study the given map of a town and select the INCORRECT option regarding it.**

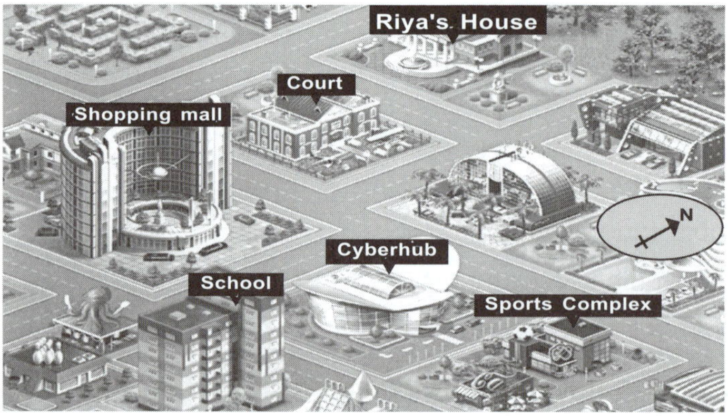

(A) Shopping mall is to the South of school.
(B) Sports complex is at East to the cyberhub.
(C) School is at South to the cyberhub.
(D) Riya's house is at North to the shopping mall.

17. **The given box contains some letters. Name of which of the following can we get from these letters?**

E T R E M V A I S D B I O

(A) An audio-visual one way mode of mass communication
(B) A means of written communication that uses internet
(C) A two way means of audio communication
(D) A means of mass communication

18. While driving, Nishi reached a point where the following road signs were present. Select the correct option regarding it.

(A) She should not take a left turn from here.
(B) There is a hospital on the right side of road.
(C) Speed limit for small vehicles like cars is 60 kmph.
(D) At a time, maximum 30 big vehicles can be allowed on this road.

DIRECTION (Q. No. 19 and 20) : Refer to the given word grid and answer the following questions.

R	V	A	M	Z	S	P	R	O
G	D	S	P	E	E	D	B	R
N	O	P	A	R	K	I	N	G
V	I	D	E	O	C	A	L	L
T	L	E	M	T	T	U	R	N
E	L	R	A	P	I	O	K	E

19. The meaning of which of the given symbols is hidden in the given word grid?

(A)  (B)  (C)  (D) 

20. The means of communication______ is hidden in this grid.

(A) Which is a two way audio means
(B) Which uses digital transmission to send written texts
(C) Which is a two way audio-visual means
(D) All of these

Darken your choice with HB Pencil

1.	Ⓐ Ⓑ Ⓒ Ⓓ	6.	Ⓐ Ⓑ Ⓒ Ⓓ	11.	Ⓐ Ⓑ Ⓒ Ⓓ	16.	Ⓐ Ⓑ Ⓒ Ⓓ
2.	Ⓐ Ⓑ Ⓒ Ⓓ	7.	Ⓐ Ⓑ Ⓒ Ⓓ	12.	Ⓐ Ⓑ Ⓒ Ⓓ	17.	Ⓐ Ⓑ Ⓒ Ⓓ
3.	Ⓐ Ⓑ Ⓒ Ⓓ	8.	Ⓐ Ⓑ Ⓒ Ⓓ	13.	Ⓐ Ⓑ Ⓒ Ⓓ	18.	Ⓐ Ⓑ Ⓒ Ⓓ
4.	Ⓐ Ⓑ Ⓒ Ⓓ	9.	Ⓐ Ⓑ Ⓒ Ⓓ	14.	Ⓐ Ⓑ Ⓒ Ⓓ	19.	Ⓐ Ⓑ Ⓒ Ⓓ
5.	Ⓐ Ⓑ Ⓒ Ⓓ	10.	Ⓐ Ⓑ Ⓒ Ⓓ	15.	Ⓐ Ⓑ Ⓒ Ⓓ	20.	Ⓐ Ⓑ Ⓒ Ⓓ

Wind helps to dry clothes, move sailboats, spread seeds to new places, etc.

- Air is all around us. Living things need air to breathe.
- Air contains water vapour, smoke, dust and germs. Excess of the last three makes air impure. Breathing impure air can make us sick.
- Moving air is called wind. Gently moving wind is called breeze and strong and damaging wind is called storm.

Weather cock indicates moving direction of wind.

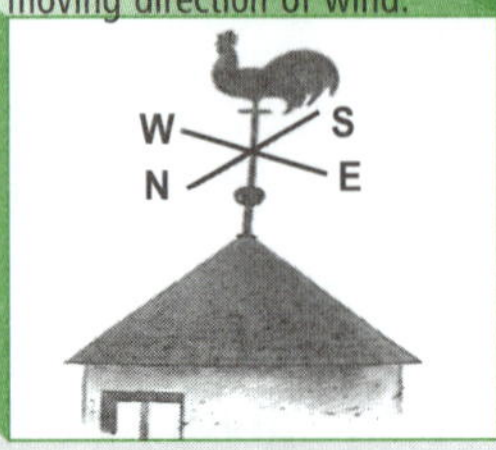

- Living things need water.
- Water comes from rain and melting of snow on mountains. Rain water fills up rivers, etc. Some of it goes deep into the soil (groundwater).
- Washing and bathing in rivers, throwing waste in it, makes the water dirty. Drinking dirty water can make us ill.

Handpumps, wells and tubewells are used to get groundwater.

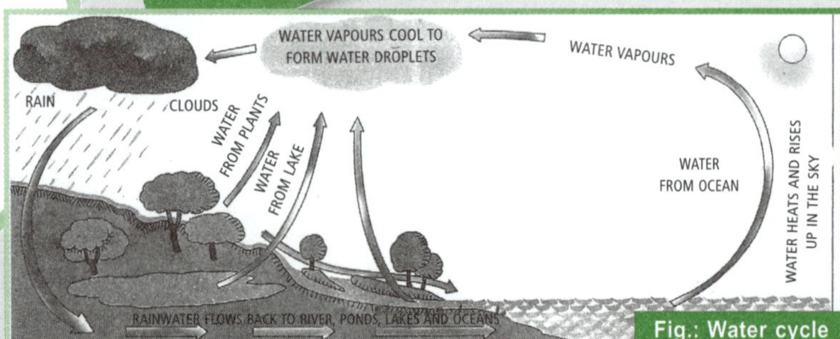

Fig.: Water cycle

- The Earth is made up of hard substances called rocks. Rocks are found under the soil, in rivers and seas.
- Rocks are of many kinds. They may be hard (granite, sand stone, etc.) or soft (coal and chalk).
- Rocks are made up of two or more minerals like mica, quartz, talc, etc. Diamond is the hardest mineral. Talc is the softest mineral.

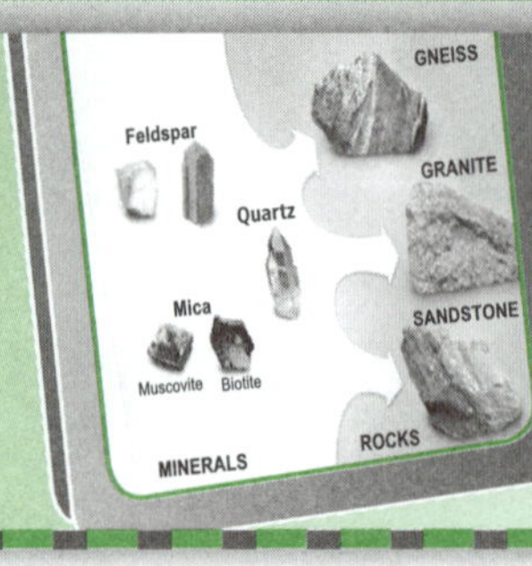

CHAPTER 10

Air, Water and Rocks

Test Skills

- ***Air and wind***
- ***Things that make air impure***
- ***Things that make water impure***
- ***Uses of air***
- ***Sources and uses of water***
- ***Rocks and minerals***

1. The activity performed by the boy in the given picture shows that ______________.

(A) Moving air has weight
(B) Moving air is needed to move things
(C) Moving air fills our surrounding
(D) All of these

2. Mrs Chauhan reuses water, which was used to wash vegetables, to water plants. She is practising _____ of water.

(A) Pollution　(B) Conservation
(C) Evaporation　(D) Desalinisation

3. Which of the following statements is INCORRECT?

(A) Precious minerals like gold and platinum are used for making jewellery.
(B) Dentists use powdered pumice for polishing our teeth.
(C) Black gold is another name of slate.
(D) Shale is used to make tiles and bricks.

4. Which among the following is the hardest mineral?

(A) Graphite　(B) Diamond
(C) Quartz　(D) Talc

5. Select the odd one out.

(A) Tubewell　(B) Well
(C) Handpump　(D) Pond

6. During storms, tin roofs of houses are blown away. It shows that_______.

(A) Air has force　(B) Air has weight
(C) Air occupies space　(D) All of these

7. **Read the given passage carefully.**
When air blows gently, it is called __X__. When air blows with great force, it is called __Y__. When wind blows very fast with thunder and lightning, it is called __Z__.
Select the option which correctly identifies X, Y and Z.

	X	Y	Z
(A)	Breeze	Wind	Storm
(B)	Wind	Storm	Breeze
(C)	Breeze	Storm	Wind
(D)	Storm	Breeze	Wind

8. **The windsock shown in the picture indicates that the wind is moving towards ______________.**

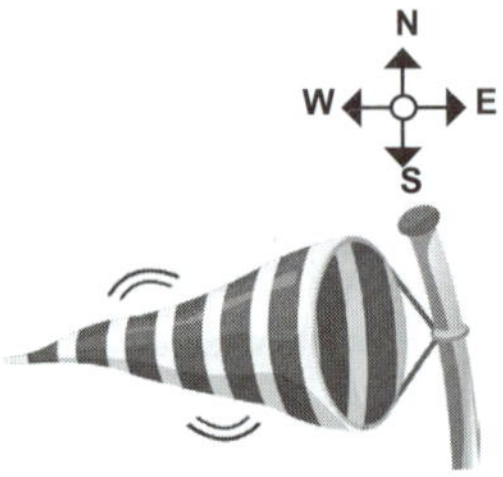

(A) North
(B) South
(C) West
(D) East

9. **Which of the following are liquid states of water?**
1. Water vapour **2. Rain**
3. Snow **4. Dew**
(A) 2 and 3 only (B) 2 and 4 only
(C) 2, 3 and 4 only (D) 1, 2, 3 and 4

10. **Water drops fall from the sky as rain. Where does all this water go ?**
1. It is absorbed into the soil.
2. The plants absorb the water.
3. It collects into the oceans and rivers.
4. It collects into the ponds and reservoirs.
(A) 1 and 2 only (B) 2 and 3 only
(C) 1 and 4 only (D) 1, 2, 3 and 4

11. **Which of the following correctly shows the water level when a beaker of water is tilted ?**

(A) (B) (C) (D)

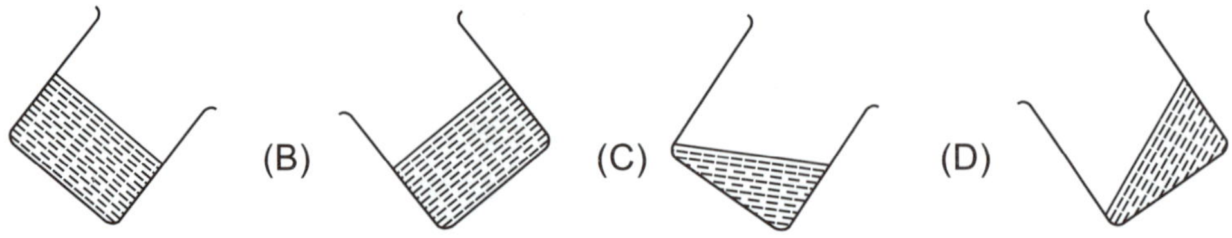

12. **Match column I with column II and select the correct option.**

	Column I		**Column II**
(a)	**Soft, black rock used as fuel**	**(i)**	**Slate**
(b)	**Rock used for making blackboards**	**(ii)**	**Talc**
(c)	**Softest mineral**	**(iii)**	**Graphite**
(d)	**Mineral used to make lead of pencils**	**(iv)**	**Coal**

(A) (a)-(ii), (b)-(i), (c)-(iii), (d)-(iv)
(B) (a)-(iv), (b)-(ii), (c)-(iii), (d)-(i)
(C) (a)-(iv), (b)-(i), (c)-(ii), (d)-(iii)
(D) (a)-(ii), (b)-(iii), (c)-(iv), (d)-(i)

13. **Which of the following products is made from the softest mineral?**

(A) 

(B) 

(C) 

(D) 

14. **Rati took a communicating vessel as shown in the figure. She filled some water in it. Which of the following correctly shows the level of water in the vessel?**

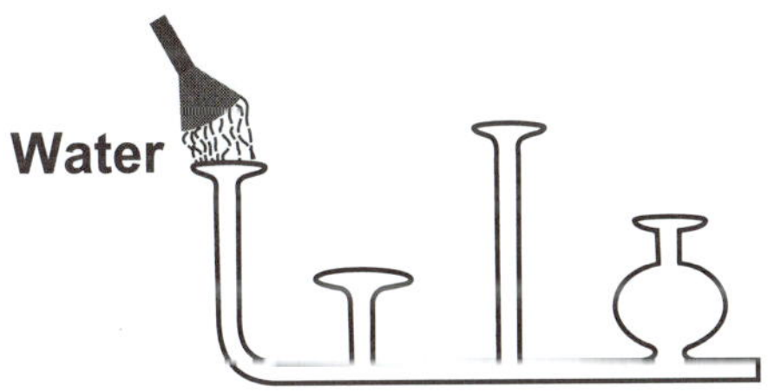

(A) 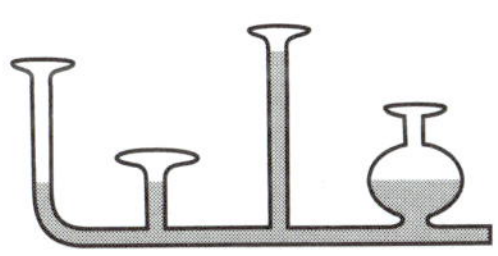

(B) 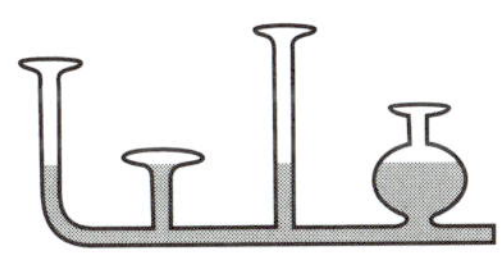

(C) 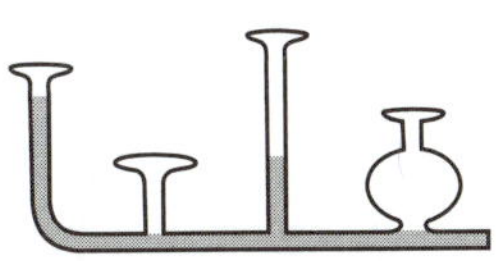

(D) 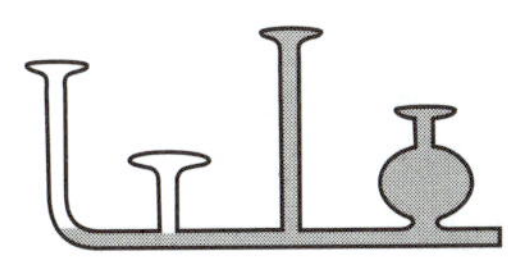

15. **The process which is also a part of the water cycle, is responsible for formation of droplets on the surface of a glass of cold drink.**
Select the option that gives the name of the above mentioned process on unscrambling.

(A) EONDACNSITON
(B) CREIPPIATITON
(C) PVAOERTIAON
(D) ATRFILTION

Achievers Section (HOTS)

16. Study the given figure showing how water is made pure before it reaches our home and identify P, Q, R and S.

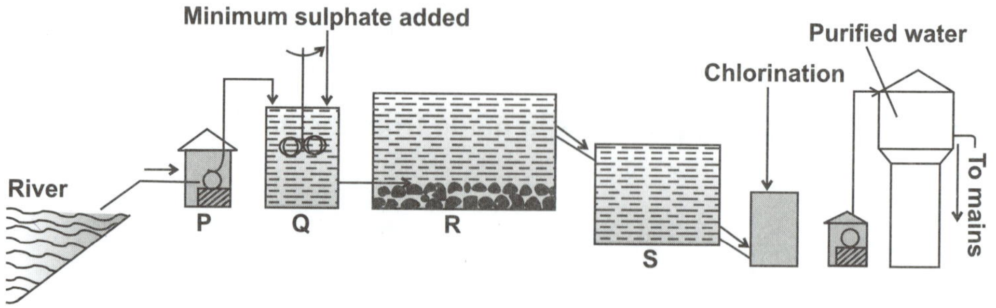

	P	Q	R	S
(A)	Mixing tank	Pump	Settling tank	Filter
(B)	Pump	Mixing tank	Settling tank	Filter
(C)	Pump	Settling tank	Mixing tank	Filter
(D)	Filter	Mixing tank	Settling tank	Pump

17. Rock X floats on water while rock Y wears easily when rubbed. Which of the following options correctly identifies these rocks?

	X	Y
(A)	Pumice	Granite
(B)	Granite	Chalk
(C)	Marble	Slate
(D)	Pumice	Chalk

DIRECTION (Q. No. 18 and 19) : Refer to the given word grid and answer the following questions.

G	O	L	P	S	S	M	R
E	B	A	N	Y	L	E	S
R	G	T	A	L	C	U	Q
M	D	I	A	M	O	N	D
S	O	Q	I	J	X	Q	Z

18. Which of the following can be found in the given grid?

(A) An object that can show that air moves things

(B) A water source that draws underground water using electricity

(C) The initiating processes of water cycle

(D) An air impurity that is a living thing

19. Two minerals X and Y are given in the word grid. X is used for making P and Y is used for making Q. Find out the rocks X and Y and then select the option that correctly identifies P and Q.

	P	**Q**
(A)	Glass cutter	Bangle
(B)	Talcum powder	Jewellery
(C)	Table top	Window pane
(D)	Ring	Anklet

20. Process X helps in drying up of wet clothes when put on clothesline under the Sun. Process Y helps in formation of cloud from water vapours present in air. Identify the processes and select the INCORRECT option regarding them.

(A) Process X is responsible for drying up of puddles and ponds during droughts.

(B) Process Y is responsible for fogging of bathroom mirror when someone takes hot shower.

(C) During process X gaseous state of water is converted into liquid state.

(D) Both processes X and Y are necessary for the completion of water cycle.

☺☺☺

Darken your choice with HB Pencil

1. Ⓐ Ⓑ Ⓒ Ⓓ	6. Ⓐ Ⓑ Ⓒ Ⓓ	11. Ⓐ Ⓑ Ⓒ Ⓓ	16. Ⓐ Ⓑ Ⓒ Ⓓ
2. Ⓐ Ⓑ Ⓒ Ⓓ	7. Ⓐ Ⓑ Ⓒ Ⓓ	12. Ⓐ Ⓑ Ⓒ Ⓓ	17. Ⓐ Ⓑ Ⓒ Ⓓ
3. Ⓐ Ⓑ Ⓒ Ⓓ	8. Ⓐ Ⓑ Ⓒ Ⓓ	13. Ⓐ Ⓑ Ⓒ Ⓓ	18. Ⓐ Ⓑ Ⓒ Ⓓ
4. Ⓐ Ⓑ Ⓒ Ⓓ	9. Ⓐ Ⓑ Ⓒ Ⓓ	14. Ⓐ Ⓑ Ⓒ Ⓓ	19. Ⓐ Ⓑ Ⓒ Ⓓ
5. Ⓐ Ⓑ Ⓒ Ⓓ	10. Ⓐ Ⓑ Ⓒ Ⓓ	15. Ⓐ Ⓑ Ⓒ Ⓓ	20. Ⓐ Ⓑ Ⓒ Ⓓ

- Our Earth is a very beautiful planet.
- It is round like a ball.
- Our Earth is the only planet known to have plants and animals on it.

- It has air and water.
- Different landforms like mountains, valleys, plains, plateaus, hills and water bodies like ocean, rivers, etc. are found on the Earth.
- Earth moves all the time. Its movement is of two types: Rotation and Revolution.
- Rotation causes day and night, while Revolution causes change in seasons.

- Moon is our closest neighbour in the sky and has mountains and valleys like Earth.
- It has no air and light of its own.
- It appears to change its shape as it moves around the Earth.

- The Sun is a huge ball of fire that gives us heat and light.
- It is our nearest star.

OUR UNIVERSE

- Stars are huge ball of fire, very very far away from us, that twinkle in the sky at night.

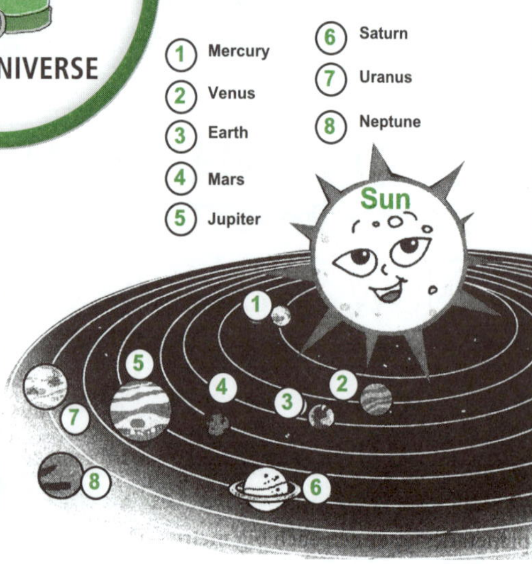

- This is our Solar System. The Sun and eight planets are the parts of the Solar System.
- These planets are round objects that move around the Sun in fixed orbits.

- Light helps us to see things around us.
- A shadow is a dark place where little or no light reaches. Anything that blocks light from passing through it, casts a shadow.

CHAPTER 11

Earth and Universe

Test Skills

- Our Solar System
- Sun, Moon and stars
- Earth and its landscape
- Day and night, light and shadow

1. Which is the smallest planet in our Solar System ?
(A) Mercury (B) Venus (C) Earth (D) Neptune

2. X is the farthest planet from the Sun in our Solar System. 'X' is ____________.
(A) Neptune (B) Uranus (C) Jupiter (D) Saturn

3. A lowland between two mountains is called ____________.
(A) Plateau (B) Hill (C) Dam (D) Valley

4. Select the correct option from the following.
(A) Unlike Moon, stars give their own light.
(B) Unlike stars, Moon gives its own light.
(C) Like Moon, stars shine by reflecting Sun's light.
(D) Like stars, Moon appears twinkling in the night sky.

5. Observe the given figure. What is the time of the day?

(A) Morning
(B) Noon
(C) Afternoon
(D) Evening

6. The day and night are caused due to ____________ of Earth on its _________.
(A) Revolution, Axis (B) Rotation, Axis
(C) Revolution, Orbit (D) Rotation, Orbit

7. Select the option that correctly identifies 'X' in the given sequence of planets.

Mercury, Venus, X, Mars

(A) Jupiter (B) Saturn (C) Neptune (D) Earth

8. **Zarrin looked at the Moon from her window. It was shining brightly in the sky. Where does the light come from, which makes the Moon shine ?**
   (A) The Moon gets its light from the Sun.
   (B) The Moon has its own light.
   (C) The Moon gets its light from satellite.
   (D) The Moon gets its light from the Earth.

9. **Select the correct match from the following.**
   (A) Valley – Small low mountain
   (B) Pond – Still water
   (C) Dam – Salty water
   (D) Ocean – Freshwater

10. **Complete the following paragraph by selecting the correct sequence of words. _____ rotates from _______ to ______ on its own ________. Its rotation causes day and night. It also revolves around the ______ on fixed path called ______.**
   (A) Earth, West, East, Axis, Sun, Orbit
   (B) Sun, East, West, Orbit, Earth, Axis
   (C) Earth, East, West, Orbit, Sun, Axis
   (D) Earth, East, West, Axis, Sun, Orbit

11. **The given diagrams show shadows of a pole at different times on a sunny day. In diagram A, the pole casts the shadow at 11.00 a.m. Predict, what time the pole will cast the shadow in diagram B.**

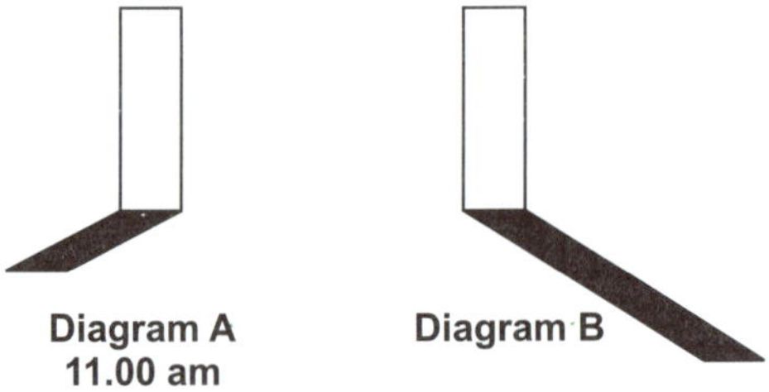

   (A) 9.00 a.m. (B) 12.00 noon
   (C) 2.00 p.m. (D) 4.00 p.m.

12. **Select the correct option regarding the figure shown here.**

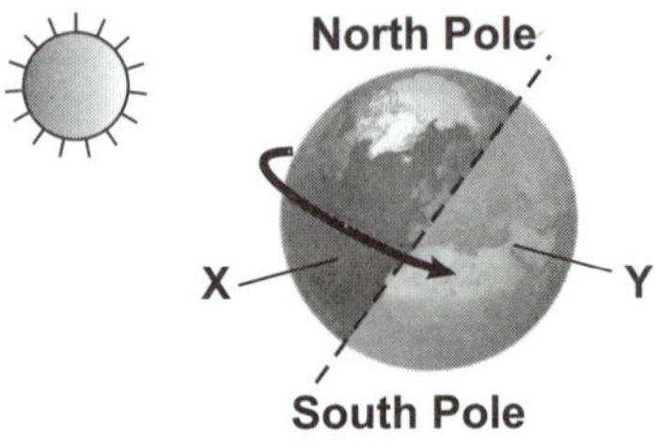

   (A) People in part X would be sleeping at this time.
   (B) People in part Y would be sleeping at this time.
   (C) People in part X would be wearing woollen clothes whereas those in part Y would be wearing only cotton clothes.
   (D) None of these

13. **____________ has no role in change of seasons at different places of Earth.**
   (A) Earth's tilt on axis (B) Rotation of Earth on its axis
   (C) Revolution of Earth in its orbit (D) All of these

14. Select the INCORRECT statement.

(A) Forests are large land areas covered with trees.

(B) Plateau is a highland which is flat on top.

(C) Hill is a small, low mountain.

(D) Pond is a large water body surrounded by land on three sides.

15. Study the table given below carefully.

Original length of a flag pole	3 m
Length of shadow of the flag pole at 8 a.m.	4 m
Length of shadow of the flag pole at 10 a.m.	2 m
Length of shadow of the flag pole at 1 p.m.	0.7 m

What will be the approximate length of the shadow at 5 p.m.?

(A) It will be longer than 4 m.

(B) It will be longer than 2 m but shorter than 4 m.

(C) It will be longer than 0.7 m but shorter than 4 m.

(D) It will be longer than 0.7 m but shorter than 2 m.

Achievers Section (HOTS)

16. Farheen drew a diagram of the Moon she saw on one night. After few nights, she drew another diagram of what the Moon looked like then. Why does the Moon look different on different nights?

(A) The Moon grows in size day by day.

(B) It comes nearer to Earth day by day.

(C) We only see that part of the Moon which is lit up by the Sun.

(D) Both (A) and (C)

17. What will be the shape of shadow formed on the wall when magnets L and K are placed between the light source and the wall as shown here?

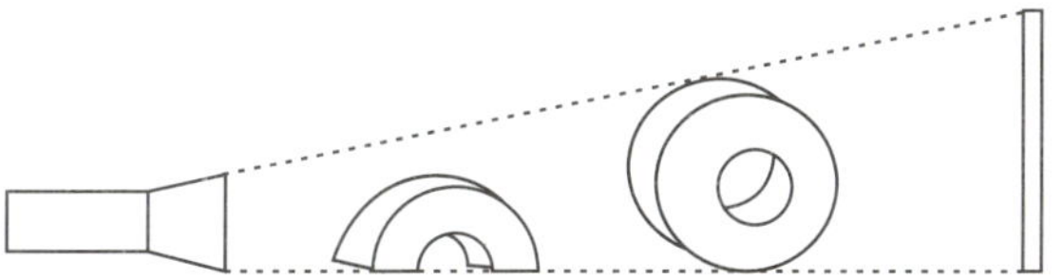

(A) 
(B) 
(C) 
(D) 

18. Supriya : Japan is called 'the land of the rising Sun'.
Vishwas : Sun is the closest star to Earth.

Read the given conversation and select the correct option.

(A) Supriya is right but Vishwas is wrong.
(B) Both Supriya and Vishwas are right.
(C) Vishwas is right but Supriya is wrong.
(D) Both Supriya and Vishwas are wrong.

19. **Vaishali fell asleep under a tree at time P and woke up at time Q (as shown). She is wondering why she cannot see her shadow. Select the correct explanation for this.**

Time P Time Q

1. **At time 'P', the tree is blocking the light and preventing it from falling on her.**
2. **At time 'Q', her shadow falls at the back, so she cannot see her shadow.**
3. **She fell asleep in the morning and woke up in the evening.**
4. **She is reflecting back sunlight.**

(A) 1 and 2 only (B) 1 and 4 only (C) 2 and 3 only (D) 3 and 4 only

20. **Select the correct option in reference to the given word chop table.**

1 MO	2 MA	3 RS	4 MER
5 AB	6 ON	7 RY	8 JU
9 ZW	10 PI	11 AR	12 CU
13 PW	14 QS	15 TER	16 SB

(A) Natural satellite of Earth – 6, 1
(B) Hottest planet of our Solar System – 4, 12, 7
(C) Smallest planet of our Solar System – 2, 3
(D) Largest planet of our Solar System – 8, 10, 15

☺☺☺

Darken your choice with HB Pencil

1.	Ⓐ Ⓑ Ⓒ Ⓓ	6.	Ⓐ Ⓑ Ⓒ Ⓓ	11.	Ⓐ Ⓑ Ⓒ Ⓓ	16.	Ⓐ Ⓑ Ⓒ Ⓓ
2.	Ⓐ Ⓑ Ⓒ Ⓓ	7.	Ⓐ Ⓑ Ⓒ Ⓓ	12.	Ⓐ Ⓑ Ⓒ Ⓓ	17.	Ⓐ Ⓑ Ⓒ Ⓓ
3.	Ⓐ Ⓑ Ⓒ Ⓓ	8.	Ⓐ Ⓑ Ⓒ Ⓓ	13.	Ⓐ Ⓑ Ⓒ Ⓓ	18.	Ⓐ Ⓑ Ⓒ Ⓓ
4.	Ⓐ Ⓑ Ⓒ Ⓓ	9.	Ⓐ Ⓑ Ⓒ Ⓓ	14.	Ⓐ Ⓑ Ⓒ Ⓓ	19.	Ⓐ Ⓑ Ⓒ Ⓓ
5.	Ⓐ Ⓑ Ⓒ Ⓓ	10.	Ⓐ Ⓑ Ⓒ Ⓓ	15.	Ⓐ Ⓑ Ⓒ Ⓓ	20.	Ⓐ Ⓑ Ⓒ Ⓓ

Logical Reasoning

1. Which box is the heaviest?

(A)  (B) 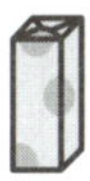 (C)  (D) 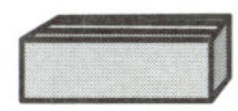

2. Which of the following clocks shows the time "half an hour after 2:40 a.m."?

(A)  (B)  (C)  (D) 

3. Find the figure from the options which will continue the same series as established by the Problem Figures.

Problem Figures

(A) 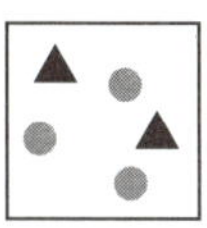 (B) 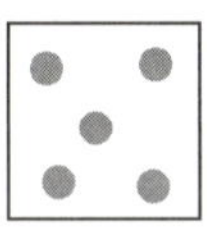 (C) 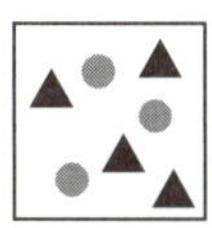 (D) 

4. Total number of sleeping, standing and slanting lines in the following figures respectively are________.

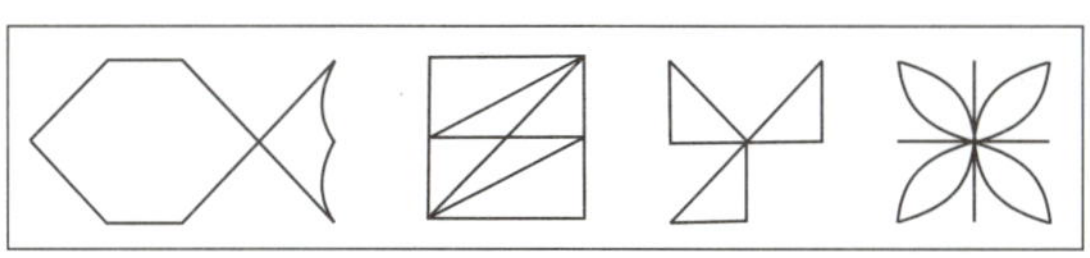

(A) 8, 6, 9 (B) 8, 6, 8 (C) 8, 7, 9 (D) 9, 6, 10

5. **Select the INCORRECT match.**

	Objects	Number of equal groups
(A)		4 of 4
(B)		2 of 5
(C)		3 of 6
(D)		5 of 2

6. **There is a certain relationship between figures (i) & (ii) and (iii) & (iv). Identify the relation and find the missing figure.**

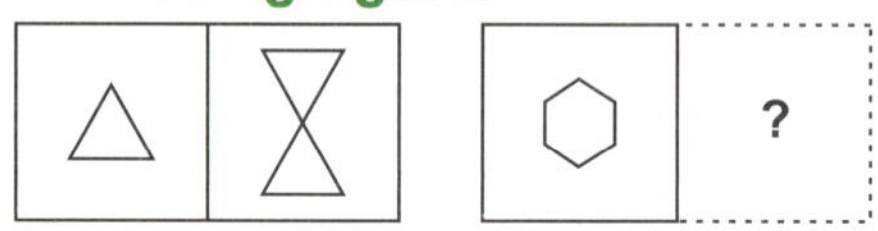

(i) (ii) (iii) (iv)

(A) 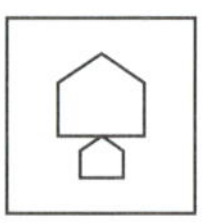 (B)  (C) 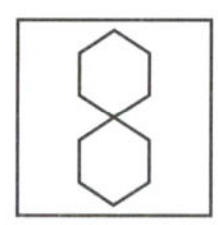 (D) 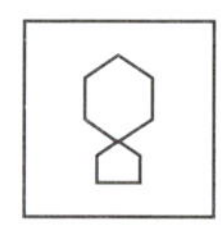

7. **Three out of four figures forms a group. Identify the figure that does not fit into the group.**

(A)  (B)  (C)  (D) 

8. **Find the figure from the options which will complete the pattern in Fig. (X).**

(A)  (B) 

(C)  (D) 

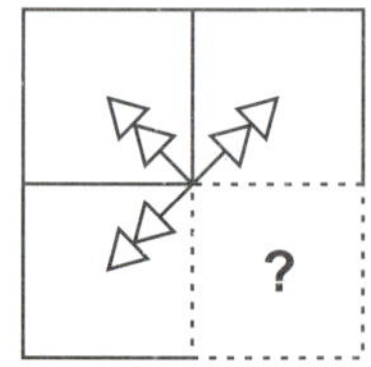

Fig. (X)

9. **Find the figure from the options in which Fig.(X) is exactly embedded as one of its part.**

Fig.(X)

(A) 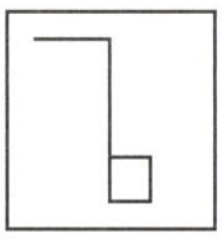 (B)  (C) 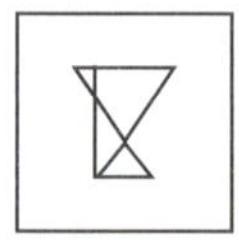 (D) 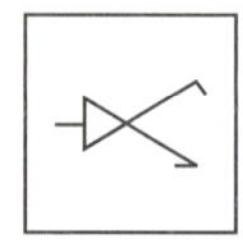

10. **There are 4 groups of _____ burgers.**

(A) 3 (B) 4 (C) 5 (D) 6

11. **How many less circles than the triangles and squares together are there in the given figure?**

(A) 2 (B) 1 (C) 3 (D) 0

12. **A jar contains 8 candies, 4 toy cars, 12 chocolates and 3 lollipops. Which of the following is least likely to come out of it?**

(A) Toy car (B) Lollipop (C) Chocolate (D) Candy

13. **Find the figure which is same as that of Fig. (X).**

Fig. (X)

(A)  (B)  (C)  (D) 

14. **Find the missing numbers.**

(A) 24, 40 (B) 25, 39 (C) 25, 29 (D) 24, 39

15. **Pawan celebrates his birthday on the next day of second Tuesday of December 20XX. On which date he celebrates his birthday?**

(A) 17th December

(B) 16th December

(C) 9th December

(D) 10th December

December 20XX						
S	M	T	W	TH	F	S
	1	2	3	4	5	6
7	8	9	10	11	12	13
14	15	16	17	18	19	20
21	22	23	24	25	26	27
28	29	30	31			

16. **Some boys are standing in a line. If Mohit and Gautam interchange their positions, then which boy will be third from the right end?**

(A) Mohit (B) Gautam (C) Raj (D) Varun

17. **How many squares and standing lines respectively are there in the given figure?**

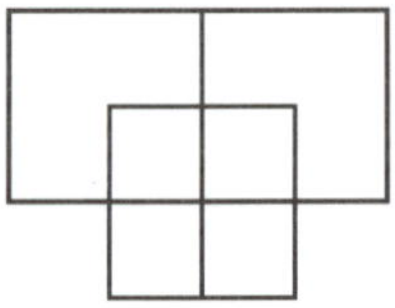

(A) 8, 11 (B) 7, 5
(C) 8, 9 (D) 5, 9

18. **There is a certain relationship between the pair of elements on the either side of ::. Identify the relation and find the missing element.**

 : 3 ::  : ?

(A) 5 (B) 2 (C) 3 (D) 4

19. **Which of the following figures is exactly embedded in Fig.(X) as one of its part?**

Fig.(X)

(A)  (B) 
(C)  (D) 

20. **In the given figure, the statue is ______  tall.**

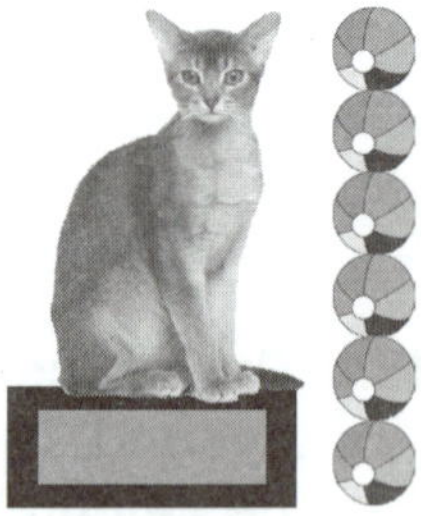

(A) 5
(B) 6
(C) 7
(D) 8

21. **If 'Apple' is called 'Mango', 'Mango' is called 'Orange', 'Orange' is called 'Grapes' and 'Grapes' is called 'Strawberry', then the king of fruits is _____.**

(A) Mango (B) Apple (C) Orange (D) Grapes

22. **Which of the following objects is longest?**

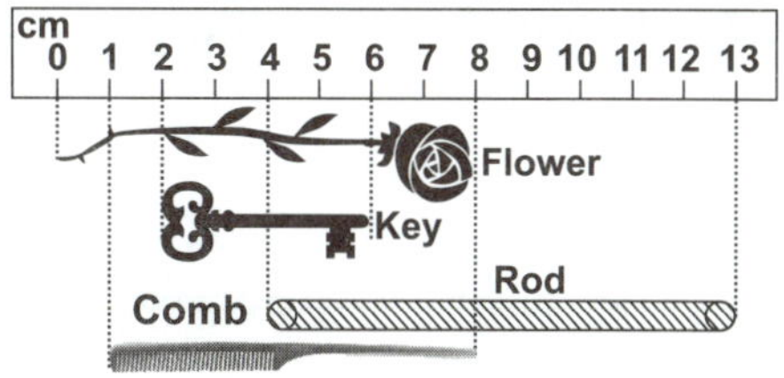

(A) Comb

(B) Key

(C) Rod

(D) Flower

23. **There is a relationship between the numbers in the first and the second rows. Identify the relation and find the values of P and Q respectively.**

First Row	20	Q	55	70
Second Row	15	10	50	P

(A) 60, 15 (B) 15, 60 (C) 15, 65 (D) 65, 15

24. **How many straight lines and curved lines are there in the given figure respectively?**

(A) 3, 5

(B) 5, 2

(C) 6, 7

(D) 5, 3

25. **Some children are standing in a line.**

P Q R S T U V W **Right**

If R and U interchange their positions, then which child will be sixth from the left end?

(A) R (B) S (C) T (D) U

26. **If**  **means** ,  **means**  **and**  **means** **, then which of the following can fly?**

(A)  (B)  (C)  (D) 

27. **In which group the given Shape (X) belongs?**

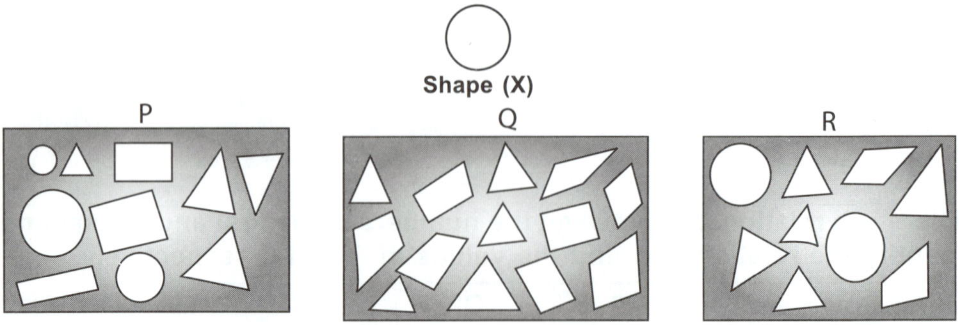

(A) P only (B) R only (C) Both P and R (D) P, Q and R

28. **How many caps will be there in pattern 5?**

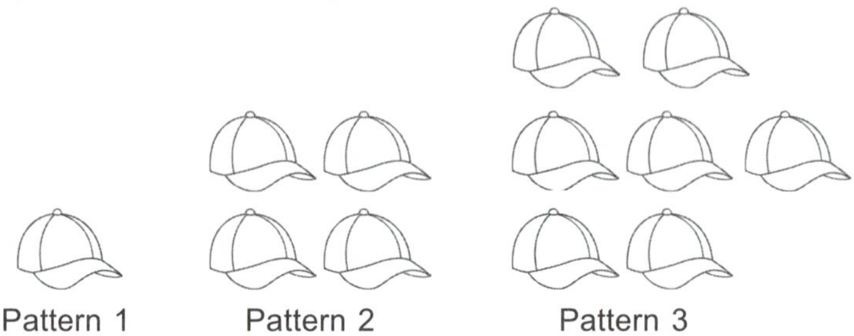

(A) 13 (B) 10 (C) 14 (D) 9

29. **Sandhya is taller than Anamika and shorter than Sanchi. Sanchi is shorter than only Monika. Who amongst them is the tallest and shortest respectively?**

(A) Sandhya, Anamika (B) Monika, Anamika
(C) Monika, Sanchi (D) Sandhya, Sanchi

30. **Kartik needs to drive to Chandigarh Via Delhi. The given figure shows the routes that he can take.**

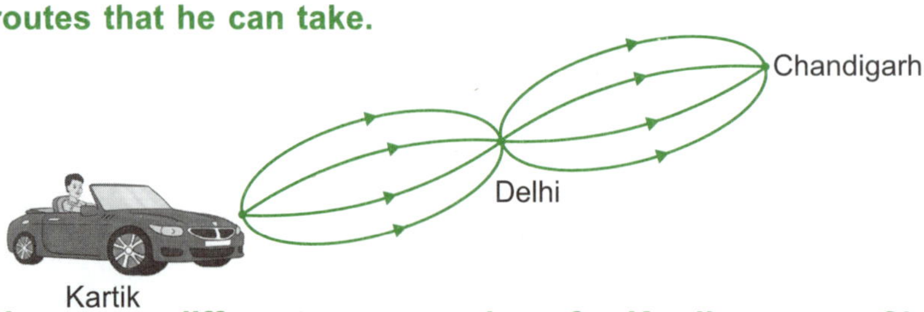

How many different ways are there for Kartik to go to Chandigarh?

(A) 20 (B) 16 (C) 12 (D) 8

31. **Which of the following costs the most?**

(A) 

(B) 

(C) 

(D) 

32. **Which of the following shapes is missing in the given figure?**

(A) Square

(B) Rectangle

(C) Triangle

(D) Circle

33. **Some girls are sitting in a line. Latika is sitting between _____ and _____.**

(A) Akansha, Preeti

(B) Kiran, Preeti

(C) Shalini, Akansha

(D) Akansha, Kiran

34. **In a certain code language, if 'MONKEY' is written as 'KEYMON', then 'ORANGE' will be written as ________.**

(A) EGNARO (B) NGEARO (C) NGEOAR (D) NGEORA

35. **Latika has collected 6 equal sized squares and 1 rectangle for her maths project. Identify the solids she would have formed with the collected material.**

(A) 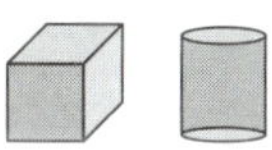 (B) 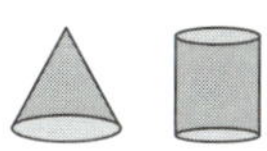 (C) 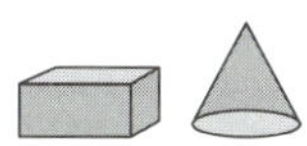 (D) 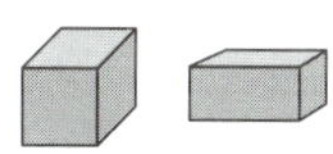

Darken your choice with HB Pencil

1.	Ⓐ Ⓑ Ⓒ Ⓓ	10. Ⓐ Ⓑ Ⓒ Ⓓ	19. Ⓐ Ⓑ Ⓒ Ⓓ	28. Ⓐ Ⓑ Ⓒ Ⓓ
2.	Ⓐ Ⓑ Ⓒ Ⓓ	11. Ⓐ Ⓑ Ⓒ Ⓓ	20. Ⓐ Ⓑ Ⓒ Ⓓ	29. Ⓐ Ⓑ Ⓒ Ⓓ
3.	Ⓐ Ⓑ Ⓒ Ⓓ	12. Ⓐ Ⓑ Ⓒ Ⓓ	21. Ⓐ Ⓑ Ⓒ Ⓓ	30. Ⓐ Ⓑ Ⓒ Ⓓ
4.	Ⓐ Ⓑ Ⓒ Ⓓ	13. Ⓐ Ⓑ Ⓒ Ⓓ	22. Ⓐ Ⓑ Ⓒ Ⓓ	31. Ⓐ Ⓑ Ⓒ Ⓓ
5.	Ⓐ Ⓑ Ⓒ Ⓓ	14. Ⓐ Ⓑ Ⓒ Ⓓ	23. Ⓐ Ⓑ Ⓒ Ⓓ	32. Ⓐ Ⓑ Ⓒ Ⓓ
6.	Ⓐ Ⓑ Ⓒ Ⓓ	15. Ⓐ Ⓑ Ⓒ Ⓓ	24. Ⓐ Ⓑ Ⓒ Ⓓ	33. Ⓐ Ⓑ Ⓒ Ⓓ
7.	Ⓐ Ⓑ Ⓒ Ⓓ	16. Ⓐ Ⓑ Ⓒ Ⓓ	25. Ⓐ Ⓑ Ⓒ Ⓓ	34. Ⓐ Ⓑ Ⓒ Ⓓ
8.	Ⓐ Ⓑ Ⓒ Ⓓ	17. Ⓐ Ⓑ Ⓒ Ⓓ	26. Ⓐ Ⓑ Ⓒ Ⓓ	35. Ⓐ Ⓑ Ⓒ Ⓓ
9.	Ⓐ Ⓑ Ⓒ Ⓓ	18. Ⓐ Ⓑ Ⓒ Ⓓ	27. Ⓐ Ⓑ Ⓒ Ⓓ	

2016 PAPER NSO

SOF NATIONAL SCIENCE OLYMPIAD

Each question in Achievers Section carries 2 marks whereas all other questions carry one mark each.

LOGICAL REASONING

1. How many groups of 5 rats can be formed from given animals?

A. 5

B. 3

C. 4

D. 2

2. Select the odd one out.

A. 

B. 

C. 

D. 

3. Trishika celebrated her birthday on 10th October 20XX. Sidak's birthday falls on the sixth day after Trishika's birthday. On which day Sidak will celebrate her birthday?

OCTOBER 20XX

S	M	T	W	Th	F	S
				1	2	3
4	5	6	7	8	9	10
11	12	13	14	15	16	17
18	19	20	21	22	23	24
25	26	27	28	29	30	31

A. 10th October

B. 15th October

C. 16th October

D. 17th October

4. Select the correct match of shaded part with corresponding shape formed.

A. 

B. 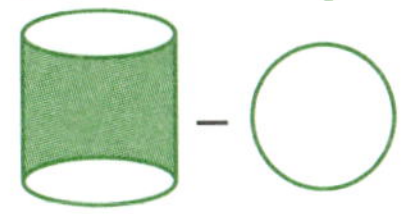

C. 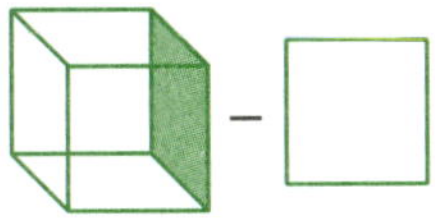

D. 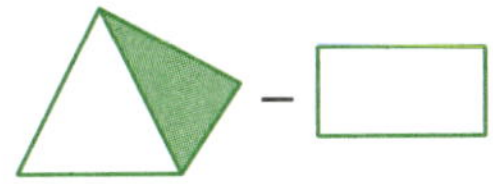

5. How many burgers will be there in pattern 5?

A. 11
B. 14
C. 17
D. 9

Pattern 1   Pattern 2   Pattern 3

SCIENCE

6. Select the group in which the odd member is INCORRECTLY encircled.

A. Kidney beans, Pea, (Tomato)
B. Brinjal, Pumpkin, (Turnip)
C. Cabbage, (Lettuce), Sugarcane
D. (Radish), Potato, Ginger

7. Match column I with column II and select the correct option.

	Column I		Column II
a.	Bee	1.	Shoes
b.	Hen	2.	Saree
c.	Camel	3.	Candle
d.	Silkworm	4.	Omelette

A. a-3, b-4, c-1, d-2
B. a-1, b-2, c-3, d-4
C. a-4, b-3, c-2, d-1
D. a-4, b-2, c-1, d-3

8. Which of the following options on unscrambling does NOT give a word related to the animal shown in picture?

A. HDSE
B. EKNELN
C. KLIM
D. ACFL

9. Select the odd one among the following.

A. 

B. 

C. 

D. 

10. Select the correct match of the leaf and fruit of a plant.

A. 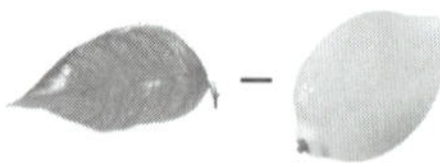

B. 

C. 

D. All of these

11. Select the option that answers the given riddle.

I have six legs. I lay eggs but I cannot fly. Who am I?

A. Spider B. Mosquito C. Housefly D. Head louse

12. Study the given diagram. Which letter represents a living thing?

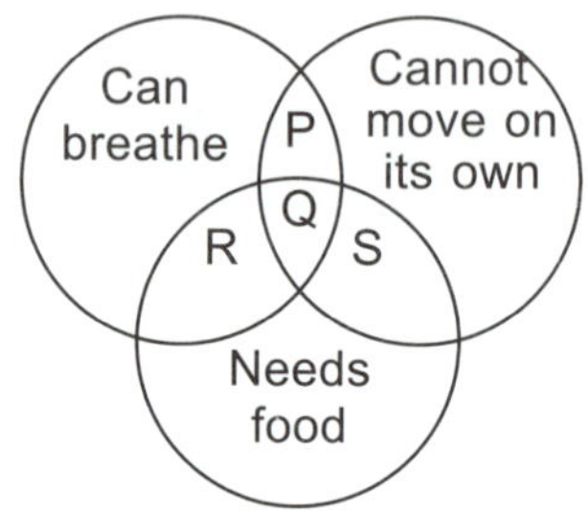

A. P

B. Q

C. R

D. S

13. Study the given flow chart and select the option which can fill the empty spaces d, e and f correctly.

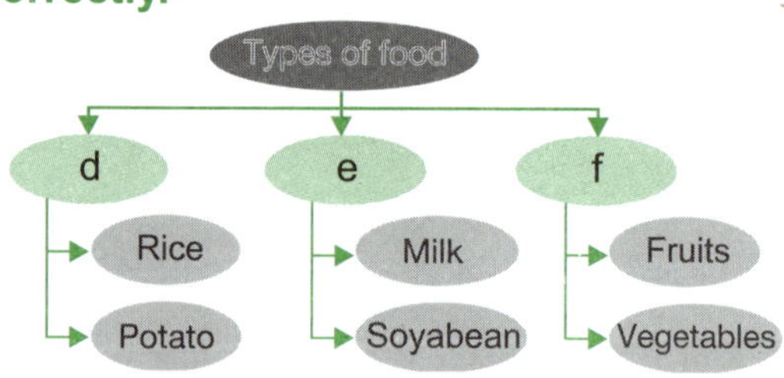

A. d-Energy giving, e-Body building, f-Protective

B. d-Protective, e-Energy giving, f-Body building

C. d-Body building, e-Protective, f-Energy giving

D. d-Energy giving, e-Protective, f-Body building

14. Ravi is ill. He feels tired all day and cannot work properly. His doctor diagnosed that there is some problem in organ X of his body, so all the other body parts are not getting sufficient oxygen. Identify organ X.

A. 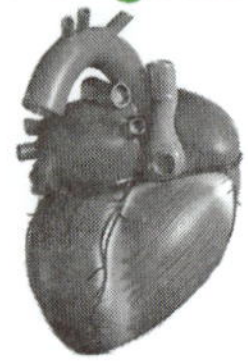

B. 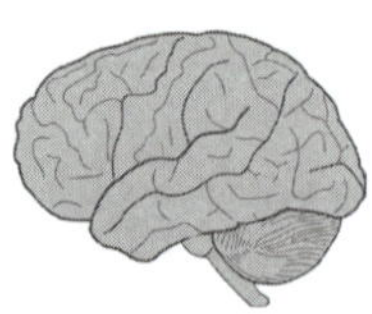

C. 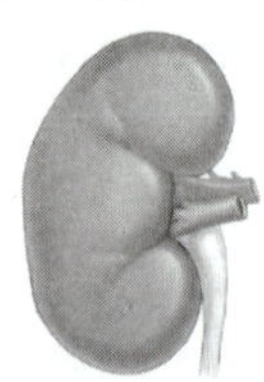

D. 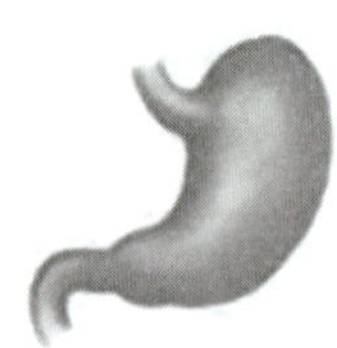

15. **The given picture shows that Ali is most likely eating his __________.**

A. Breakfast

B. Lunch

C. Dinner

D. Any of these

16. **In a state of our country, it rains almost daily and heavily. Which of the following types of house will be preferably found there?**

A.  B.  C.  D. 

17. **Weather forecast of a place on a particular day is shown here. The clothes made of fibres obtained from which of the following will be suitable for wearing on this day?**

DD-MM-YYYY	

Temp. : 35°C	
Sunrise	5:45 am
Sunset	6:00 pm

A. Cotton plant

B. Sheep

C. Yak

D. Rubber tree

18. **Which of the following are benefits of outdoor activities?**
    1. **They help in bonding with people.**
    2. **They give physical benefits and help in keeping fit.**
    3. **They increase stress and challenges of life.**

A. 1 and 2 only B. 2 and 3 only C. 1 and 3 only D. 1, 2 and 3

19. **Manu wants to fly a kite. Look at the picture and identify the correct direction in which he should fly the kite.**

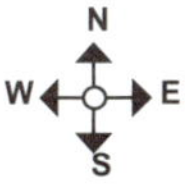

A. East

B. West

C. North

D. South

20. **Select the option that correctly arranges the given rocks in ascending order of hardness.**

A. Granite > Sandstone > Chalk B. Chalk < Sandstone < Granite

C. Pumice < Marble < Slate D. Slate > Pumice > Marble

21. **Read the following statements made by Sunita and Mohan.**

Sunita : I need bread, butter, eggs, cup cakes, etc. **Mohan : I need medicines.**

Where should Sunita and Mohan go to buy the things they need?

	Sunita	**Mohan**		**Sunita**	**Mohan**
A.	Chemist	Bakery	B.	Bakery	Chemist
C.	Stationery shop	Chemist	D.	Grocery shop	Bakery

22. **Refer to the given picture. What time of the day does it show?**

A. Evening
B. Noon
C. Morning
D. Cannot be predicted

23. **Unscramble the given words to find out the item which can be present in the given room of the house.**

A. VEON
B. BUCETK
C. OATTSER
D. ILPLOW

24. **Select the option that will correctly complete the word given in bold in the following statement.**
We need to wear W_ _ L _ E _ clothes when temperature is low.

A. OULN B. OOEN C. OOLN D. OOLY

25. **Select the bad habit from the following.**

A. We should never touch any electrical gadget with wet hands.
B. We must eat food slowly.
C. We must not get in or out of a moving bus.
D. We should eat food from outside vendors.

26. **When Ram got hurt in the school playground while playing, his friends did the following things:**

Ruchi : Started crying	**Shivi : Ran away**	**Sonu : Called the teacher**

Which child did the right thing?

A. Ruchi B. Shivi
C. Sonu D. Both Ruchi and Shivi

27. **Select the INCORRECT match.**

A. Urgent messages – Letters B. Telephone – STD, ISD
C. Internet – E-mail D. Picture news – TV

28. First aid is the ________.

A. Activity done on the first day of school
B. Immediate help given to an injured person before the doctor is available
C. First tooth erupted in a baby's mouth
D. Student who leads school sports team

29. Air keeps a fire burning. This feature of air turns dangerous when it helps ________.

A. A candle to burn on a birthday cake
B. Bonfire to burn during Lohri celebration
C. Fire in a tree to spread to other trees of forest
D. In cooking food on a stove

30. Select the correct match from the following.

A. Valley – Small low mountain
B. Pond – Still water
C. Dam – Salty water
D. Ocean – Freshwater

ACHIEVERS SECTION

31. Refer to the given family tree and select the correct option regarding it.

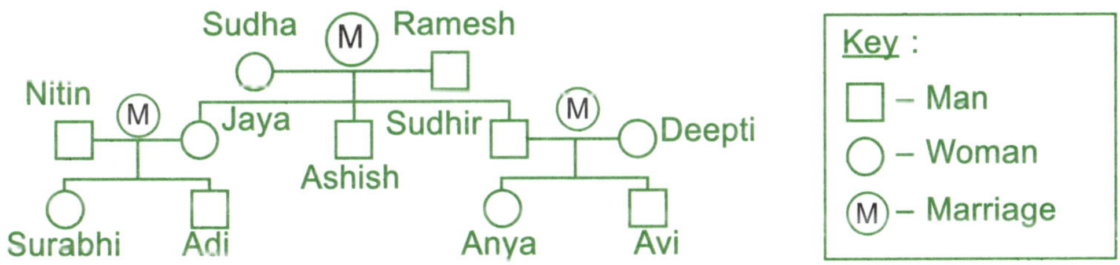

A. Sudha has four grand-daughters.
B. Ramesh has one married and one unmarried son.
C. Jaya is sister-in-law of Ashish, Sudhir and Deepti.
D. Surabhi is second cousin of Anya and Avi.

32. Refer to the given figure of water cycle and select the INCORRECT option regarding it.

A. Process P is also involved in drying of clothes.
B. Process Q is not necessary in the completion of water cycle and process R can directly follow process P.
C. An increase in process R can lead to floods.
D. Process Q is also observed when small droplets of water are seen on a glass of cold drink.

33. The given diagram shows four different places P, Q, R and S on the Earth. Select the correct match of travel path and the transport means that can be used to travel it.

A. PQ - Ship only
B. PR - Bus only
C. RS - Aeroplane or Ship
D. SQ - Aeroplane only

34. Ruhi observed the shadows of two poles on the ground at different times of the day and noted their length in a table. If the pole P is of 2 metres(m) in height then what will be the height of pole Q?

A. 2 m
B. 3 m
C. 4 m
D. Cannot be determined

Time	Shadow length	
	Pole P	Pole Q
7.00 AM	3 m	6 m
12.00 PM	0 m	0 m
4.00 PM	2.5 m	5 m

35. Names of some professionals are hidden in the given word grid.

a. How many names are hidden?

b. How many of them require skills for the work and not high education?

N	T	A	F	T	S	S	N
O	A	B	A	R	B	E	R
A	I	S	R	C	H	E	H
P	L	U	M	B	E	R	N
P	O	R	E	H	G	I	A
Q	R	V	R	I	K	B	A

	a	b
A.	Four	Two
B.	Five	Three
C.	Four	Four
D.	Three	Two

☺☺☺

Darken your choice with HB Pencil

1.	Ⓐ Ⓑ Ⓒ Ⓓ	10.	Ⓐ Ⓑ Ⓒ Ⓓ	19.	Ⓐ Ⓑ Ⓒ Ⓓ	28.	Ⓐ Ⓑ Ⓒ Ⓓ
2.	Ⓐ Ⓑ Ⓒ Ⓓ	11.	Ⓐ Ⓑ Ⓒ Ⓓ	20.	Ⓐ Ⓑ Ⓒ Ⓓ	29.	Ⓐ Ⓑ Ⓒ Ⓓ
3.	Ⓐ Ⓑ Ⓒ Ⓓ	12.	Ⓐ Ⓑ Ⓒ Ⓓ	21.	Ⓐ Ⓑ Ⓒ Ⓓ	30.	Ⓐ Ⓑ Ⓒ Ⓓ
4.	Ⓐ Ⓑ Ⓒ Ⓓ	13.	Ⓐ Ⓑ Ⓒ Ⓓ	22.	Ⓐ Ⓑ Ⓒ Ⓓ	31.	Ⓐ Ⓑ Ⓒ Ⓓ
5.	Ⓐ Ⓑ Ⓒ Ⓓ	14.	Ⓐ Ⓑ Ⓒ Ⓓ	23.	Ⓐ Ⓑ Ⓒ Ⓓ	32.	Ⓐ Ⓑ Ⓒ Ⓓ
6.	Ⓐ Ⓑ Ⓒ Ⓓ	15.	Ⓐ Ⓑ Ⓒ Ⓓ	24.	Ⓐ Ⓑ Ⓒ Ⓓ	33.	Ⓐ Ⓑ Ⓒ Ⓓ
7.	Ⓐ Ⓑ Ⓒ Ⓓ	16.	Ⓐ Ⓑ Ⓒ Ⓓ	25.	Ⓐ Ⓑ Ⓒ Ⓓ	34.	Ⓐ Ⓑ Ⓒ Ⓓ
8.	Ⓐ Ⓑ Ⓒ Ⓓ	17.	Ⓐ Ⓑ Ⓒ Ⓓ	26.	Ⓐ Ⓑ Ⓒ Ⓓ	35.	Ⓐ Ⓑ Ⓒ Ⓓ
9.	Ⓐ Ⓑ Ⓒ Ⓓ	18.	Ⓐ Ⓑ Ⓒ Ⓓ	27.	Ⓐ Ⓑ Ⓒ Ⓓ		

HINTS & EXPLANATIONS

1 Plants

1. **(D) :** Food grains are small dry seeds which are grown by human beings for food, *e.g.*, wheat, rice, maize, barley, gram and pulses.

2. **(A) :** Gum is made from the juice of Acacia (keekar) tree.

3. **(C) :** The plant shown here is bamboo plant. The pulp of its stem is used to make paper.

4. **(D) :** The pair in the box is of shrub and creeper. Similarly, in option 'D', mehendi is a shrub and watermelon is a creeper.

5. **(A) :** The plants shown here are spinach plant, mustard plant, groundnut plant and coconut plant. Out of these, spinach plant does not yield any oil.

6. **(A) :** We eat stem of yam while we eat green leaves of spinach, cabbage and mint.

7. **(B) :** In the given figure, W is leaf, X is flower, Y is root and Z is stem. Flowers give rise to fruits that bear seeds inside them.

8. **(A) :** Water is absorbed by roots and moves to upper parts of plant's body. Water also evaporates from leaves. It is neither taken up by leaves ('B' and 'C') from the air nor released from roots ('C' and 'D') to the soil.

9. **(B) :** Sameer is describing cotton plant. Jute and coconut produce rough fibres while money plant does not produce fibres.

10. **(C)**

11. **(C) :** A plant starts its life from a seed as seedling. The seedling develops leaves and its stem produces new branches to develop into a young plant. A young plant grows in height and produces new leaves but no flowers till it is young. When the plant matures, *i.e.,* becomes adult, it starts producing flowers. A plant has roots, stem, and needs air right from the beginning of life till the end.

12. **(B) :** A banyan plant can live for hundreds of years, rose plant lives for a few years while rice plant has a life of only few months.

13. **(A) :** Leaves are called food factories of plant because they make food for plant. Roots anchor the plant to soil and absorb the nutrients and water from the soil which is used by plant to make its food. The stem transports this water and the food prepared by leaves to all other parts.

14. **(A) :** Rubber is made from stem juice of the rubber plant, which is a tree not a shrub.

15. **(B) :** Clove and mustard are medicinal plants that are also used as spices.

16. **(C) :** The flowers shown are of rose and China rose. Both plants are shrubs, so they have woody stems. As these plants bear flowers, so they produce seeds also.

17. **(B) :** Coconut is a plant with trunk that means it is a tree. We get coconut oil from it. Sunflower is a herb with soft stem. It also provides us oil. Mustard and groundnut also produce oil but they are not trees, they are herbs.

18. **(C) :** Shrubs are smaller than trees. They have woody stem and their branches grow close to the ground, e.g., cotton, China rose, etc. In the given flow chart, 'd' is a tree, 'e' is a shrub, 'f' is a herb, 'g' is a climber and 'h' can be a creeper. Coconut is a tree and coriander is a herb.

19. **(B) :** In the given figure P, Q, R and S represent flower, leaf, stem and root,

respectively. Not all flowers are good to eat, but broccoli and cauliflower are the flowers that are edible (can be eaten). Groundnut is an edible seed, cabbage is edible leaf and potato is a modified stem.

20. **(B)**

2 Animals

1. **(B) :** We should not hurt animals. We should be kind to them as they are also living beings like us.

2. **(D)** 3. **(A)**

4. **(C) :** Moo, Moo is the sound of cow and cow gives us milk.

5. **(C) :** The table consists of animals and their homes. Pigeon lives in a nest and hens are kept in a coop.

6. **(D) :** Snake, tiger and sheep live on land while fish lives only in water.

7. **(D)**

8. **(D) :** Wool is obtained from fur of sheep, yak and rabbit (option A). Cow, goat and buffalo give us milk (option B). We eat eggs of birds like hen, duck and goose. Their flesh is also eaten (option C). Elephant and mule both help humans by carrying loads while crocodile skin is used to make leather (option D). Hence, option 'D' is the group with mistake, as these animals are useful to us in different ways, not in similar way.

9. **(D)**

10. **(A) :** The home of the dog is called KENNEL (option A). Pig lives in STY (option B). Horse lives in STABLE (option C) whereas honeybee lives in a HIVE (option D).

11. **(A) :** Giraffe would be called as prey animal. Prey is an animal that is killed and eaten by another animals such as lion in the given case.

12. **(C)**

13. **(C) :** We get wool which is used to make sweater (1) from sheep, yak, rabbit, etc. We get leather which is used to make handbags (2) from camel, snake, crocodile, etc. We get silk used to make silk saree (3) from silkworm.

14. **(B) :** Elephant's young one is called calf, that we get from option (B) ~~M~~ C ~~N~~ A ~~C~~ L ~~P~~ F ~~O~~. Option (A) gives LAMB, Option (C) gives KID and option (D) gives CUB.

15. **(C)**

16. **(C) :** Crowding effects can be seen by changing number of fish in water while keeping other factors as constant.

17. **(C) :** Peacock is a bird that can fly. Louse is an insect that cannot fly.

18. **(D) :** Bear is a wild animal that eats both flesh and plants. Zebra is a wild animal that eats plants only. Lion is a wild animal that eats flesh only.

19. **(C) :** According to the poem 'X' lives in water (pond) and 'Y' hops in the field and over water. Hence, 'X' is fish that lives in pond and 'Y' is kangaroo that hops.

20. **(B) :** Deer and zebra, both are wild animals that eat plants, so they cannot be P. Cow gives us milk and its young one is called calf. It is a domestic animal that eats plants. R can be vulture but S cannot be hyena as it is also a scavenger.

3 Human Body

1. **(A) :** Correct posture is very important to keep the body healthy, therefore, we should never lie down while reading. We should always sit straight while reading.

2. **(C)**

3. **(D) :** The place where two or more bones (not muscles) join together is called joint.

4. **(C) :** We use our eyes to see different things like the shining raindrops on leaves.

5. **(A) :** Lungs are the breathing organs. The air we take in through nose reaches our lungs. If a person has difficulty in breathing, it means that he has some problem in his lungs.

6. **(C) :** Heart is a small, muscular organ present inside our chest that pumps blood to all other body parts.

7. **(D) :** Activities like walking, jogging, stretching, rope skipping, etc., work on our muscles and make them strong.

8. **(B)** 9. **(B)** 10. **(D)** 11. **(C)**

12. **(B) :** Jogging, running and rope skipping make our leg muscles strong. Playing badminton makes both leg and arm muscles strong.

13. **(C) :** The options on unscrambling give EARS, EYES, NOSE and SKIN, respectively. Neetu must have used her nose to sense the smell of burning rice.

14. **(D)**

15. **(C) :** Skin helps us to feel if something is hot, cold, soft, smooth, rough or hard.

16. **(C) :** Aman can use his tongue to differentiate between orange juice and water. With the help of hands (skin) he can differentiate between round ball and a rectangular box. With the help of his ears he can differentiate between empty piggy bank and a piggy bank with some coins in it by the sound made by coins on shaking the piggy bank.

17. **(B) :** Garima used her hands (skin) to feel the texture of hair. This will also help her in differentiating between hot coffee and cold drink.

18. **(C) :** Pupil 'C' has his mouth tied so he cannot taste the coffee to know if it is sweet or not.

19. **(C) :** Heart is the organ that pumps blood in our body. It is not a sense organ.

20. **(B) :** The given word grid contains two sense organs that are eye and ear and two internal organs that are heart and lung.

4 Food

1. **(D) :** Mango is used for making *aam panna*, lemon is used for making lemonade and coffee beans are used in making coffee.

2. **(C) :** We should avoid eating uncovered and unhygienic food items from roadside vendors as they can make us sick.

3. **(B)**

4. **(D) :** Egg, fish and milk are body building foods while bread is an energy giving food.

5. **(D) :** Breakfast should be heavy because body needs energy after long gap between meals (during sleep) and to start a new day full of work. Dinner should be light because after having it we sleep and digestion slows down.

6. **(B) :** Sprouts are rich in nutrients and are good for our health while potato chips, french fries and burgers are junk foods.

7. **(A)**

8. **(B) :** Pickling preserves food by killing microbes as a result of salty and oily environment. In jellying, excess of sugar is added to food to preserve it for longer time.

9. **(A) :** Balanced diet is a diet that contains all the nutrients in right amount. For a balanced diet, we must take some food from each group (given in the options A, B, C and D) in every meal. Sugar, butter and oil should be consumed in least amount as excess of these food items can be harmful for our health.

10. **(D) :** Milk and milk products are rich sources of calcium. Therefore, missing them in diet will eventually result in weak bones and teeth.

11. **(C) :** We should not eat junk foods because they are unhealthy and overeating of junk foods may result in diseases. We should eat food at regular intervals everyday, as it helps in proper digestion of food.

12. **(C)**

13. **(D) :** Soybean and cheese are body building foods. Jaggery is energy giving food whereas vegetables are protective food.

14. **(D)**

15. **(B) :** Fish, eggs and pulses are body-building foods. Therefore, they will help Amol to develop strong muscles required for being a sportsperson.

16. **(B) :** Rice provides us energy, egg helps in body building and nuts are protective food.

17. **(B) :** Keeping food at low temperature prevents it from being spoiled by germs. Therefore, fish frozen in ice can stay unspoiled for a long time.

18. **(B) :** Bread and butter are energy rich foods while sprouts are body building food.

19. **(A) :** Milk is considered as vegetarian food item because it does not involve killing of animals. Butter, milk, cheese, etc., are vegetarian food items (R) from animals sources.

20. **(D) :** FREEZING is the technique hidden in the given word grid that includes preserving food at low temperatures.

5 Housing and Clothing

1. **(D)**

2. **(A) :** Sheep and some other animals like mountain goat, etc., give us woollen fibres which are used to make warm clothes.

3. **(D) :** Snow slides off the sloping roofs, hence does not collect on it.

4. **(B) :** Igloos are special houses made of snow blocks. They are made by Eskimo people that live in North Pole.

5. **(C) :** Nomads live in temporary houses like tents, caravans, etc.

6. **(D) :** We get the word 'silk' by unscrambling the letters in the box. Option 'D' is a silk saree.

7. **(A) :** Kunal is sleeping at this time and we sleep in the bedroom.

8. **(A) :** Houses are made on stilts at places where it rains a lot so that even if the water collects on the ground, it does not enter the houses and the houses remain dry.

9. **(D) :** Name of igloo (D) is not hidden in the puzzle. Igloo is a house made of ice. Option 'A' is a houseboat, 'B' is a caravan and 'C' is a tent.

10. **(C) :** Knitting is the process of making cloth from wool yarn.

11. **(B)**

12. **(A) :** Sloping roof and houses made of wood can be found commonly in both types of areas.

13. **(B) :** The things shown in the box X are mug, soaps and toothpaste. These things are found in the bathroom.

    B ~~A~~ R T H ~~O~~ R O O ~~O~~ M

    Option 'A' is kitchen, 'C' is bedroom and 'D' is living room,

14. **(D) :** Bungalow is not a temporary house. Stilt houses can be found in hilly areas with snowfall. Sloping roofs are not found in all permanent houses.

15. **(B) :** 'X' is cotton. Clothes made from cotton are not suitable to be worn in winter because they cannot keep us warm. Cotton clothes keep us cool.

16. **(B) :** 'f' is caravan, a temporary house on wheels and 'h' is igloo, a temporary house made of ice.

17. **(A) :** Weather forecast predicts 3rd July 20XX to be a rainy day. Raincoat should be worn or carried on 3rd July 20XX, as it will protect from rain.

18. **(B)**

19. **(D) :** Woollen fibres entrap air to keep us warm and burn with the smell of burning hair because they are made from hair of animals like sheep, etc.

20. **(C) :** The cloth piece 'Q' has not absorbed any water, it shows that the cloth material 'Q' is waterproof. Thus, it would be most suitable to make a raincoat.

6 Family and Festivals

1. **(D) :** Indoor activities are those activities that are played inside the house. Carrom, chess and table tennis are played inside the house.

2. **(C) :** In the given picture we can see groom sitting on a horse and his friends and relatives dancing and enjoying in a 'barat'. This occasion is a wedding.

3. **(C) :** A surname is a family name common to all members of a family. A nickname is an informal name given to us by close persons like parents, etc.

4. **(A) :** Samadhi is a memorial built at the burial or cremation place of somebody. Our Rashtrapita Mahatma Gandhi's samadhi is known as Raj Ghat.

5. **(B) :** Eid is a festival celebrated by muslims. On this occasion they wear new clothes, offer prayer at mosque and eat *meethi sewaian*.

6. **(B) :** Two persons married to each other are called spouse and male is called husband while the female is called wife.

7. **(D) :** Ludo, carrom and chess all are indoor activities while football is an outdoor activity.

8. **(A)**

9. **(A) :** Outdoor activities do not increase stress and challenges of life but they bring us joy.

10. **(D) :** As a member of family, we should do our household chores, help our elders and obey them.

11. **(D)**

12. **(A) :** Mr X is a sikh as sikhs wear turban and follow Guru Gobind Singh. Sikhs go to gurdwara to offer prayers.

13. **(B) :** Table tennis is an indoor game while polo is an outdoor game.

14. **(D) :** Son of sister is called nephew. Grandmother's sister is also called grandmother. Son of mother's uncle is uncle not cousin.

15. **(B) :** Festival shown in the given picture is Eid. It is celebrated by muslims. Special prayers are offered in mosques on this day. They wear new clothes and eat *meethi sewaian*.

16. **(A) :** Huge effigies of King Ravana along with his brother Kumbhkaran and son Meghnath are burnt on Dussehra every year.

17. **(B) :**

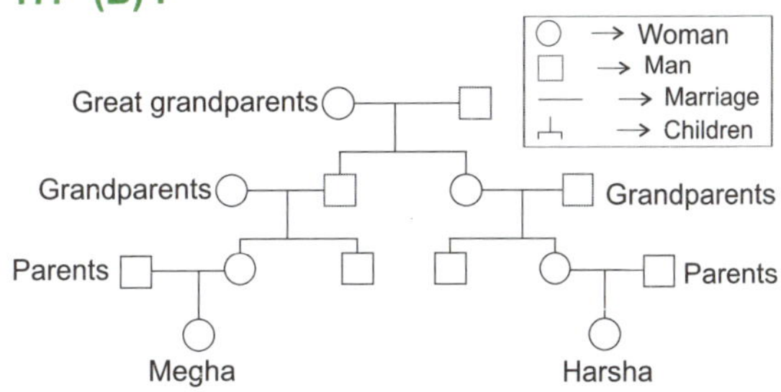

It is clear from the above chart that Megha and Harsha are second cousins.

18. **(C) :** As Rajeev and Shweta are siblings, therefore Latika (daughter of Shweta) would be Rajeev's niece. Rajeev and Sudesh are siblings. Garima is Sudesh's niece and Amit is Kapil's grandson.

19. **(C) :** In a family tree, a sleeping line between a man and a woman denotes a marriage and standing line denotes children, branches that arise from this standing line denote the number of children.
According to the above set of rules, Shalini's family tree can be interpreted as :

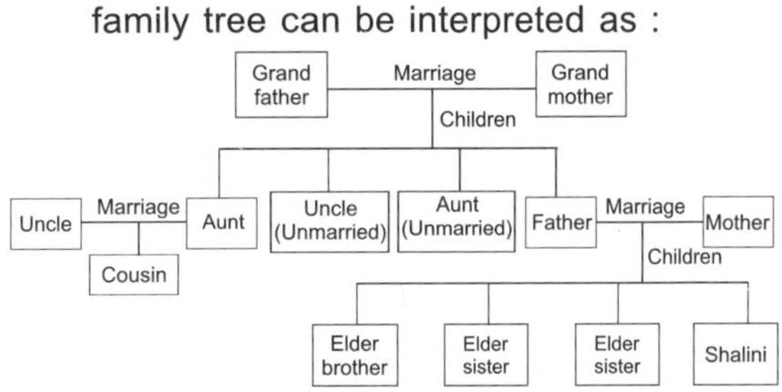

Now, it is clear that Shalini has one cousin sister, one elder brother and two elder sisters, and her grandfather has two daughters and two sons.

20. (B) : Christmas is the festival that marks birthday of Jesus Christ. Holi is the festival of colours.

7 Occupations

1. (D) : A carpenter repairs and makes wooden furnitures like table, bed, etc.

2. (D)

3. (B) : The person shown in the picture is a policeman.

4. (A) : Plumber is the professional who installs and fixes water pipes, taps, etc.

5. (D) : Mending (repairing) of shoes is done by cobbler.

6. (D) : Painter, mason and architect are related to each other as they work together for making a building. Barber has no role in it. He cuts hair.

7. (C) : Option 'C' is a stethoscope which is used by doctors to listen to the heartbeat of patients.

8. (D) : The carpenter makes wooden goods and the plumber fits and repairs pipes, taps, etc.

9. (D) : Khurpi (option 'A'), plough (option 'B') and sickle (option 'C') are used by farmer.

10. (C) : Raju is hurt so, he should go to a doctor to get his wound cleaned and dressed properly. Doctor may prescribe some medicines (to reduce pain and for quick recovery) which he can then buy from a chemist.

11. (D)

12. (B) : For paneer, one should go to a grocer.

13. (B) : A stationer is the professional who sells stationery items like notebooks, pencils, pens, etc.

14. (C) : Greengrocer sells vegetables, grocer sells items of daily needs like spices, etc. and farmer grows plants that provide spices, vegetables, etc. in his farm.

15. (D) : A bank employee can accept deposits from public and can give loans to the customers. Sending and receiving telegrams and money orders is done by the postman.

16. (D) : The given figure shows a post office.

17. (A) : The professional shown here is an architect.

18. (C) : An architect is a person who designs buildings. He needs pencil, scale and paper for it. A mason is a person who is skilled in constructing buildings with bricks, cement and water. 'd' is a carpenter, 'f' is a painter and 'g' is an electrician.

19. (C) : Tool (C) is cobbler stand used by cobbler for mending shoes. Tool (A) is hammer which is used by a carpenter, tool (B) is trowel which is used by a mason, farmer etc. and tool (D) is plier which is used by an electrician or plumber.

20. (C) : The names of professionals hidden in the given word grid can be identified as TAILOR, FARMER, BARBER and PLUMBER. All of these require skills for the work and not high education.

8 Good Habits and Safety Rules

1. (B) : First aid is the immediate help given to a person who is hurt, before the doctor comes. It involves cleaning of wound, preventing blood flow, tying broken bones to prevent further damage, etc.

2. (A) : We should eat small quantities of food at a time. Stuffing the mouth with food can lead to choking.

3. (C) : One should always walk on the footpath. If footpath is not there, then walk on the sides. Use a subway (underground path) or zebra crossing or footbridge whichever is present to cross the road.

4. (D) : We should use proper safety gears while swimming like swimming float, swimming goggles, etc. Helmet is used as a safety gear while driving or horse riding, etc.

5. **(D) :** We should never fly kite alone on a terrace with no railings because we can fall down easily and can get hurt.

6. **(D) :** We should never play with fire objects and objects with sharp edges like blades, knives, etc. as they can hurt us.

7. **(D) :** In case your friend gets hurt while playing, you should not panic, instead you should call the nearest available adult for help.

8. **(B)**

9. **(C) :** A child should not go for swimming alone. As a beginner one should use swimming tube and swim with grown-up. Children should swim in the shallow end.

10. **(B) :** We should not play with burners in the kitchen as this can cause serious injury to us.

11. **(C) :** For cleaning nose one should use tissue or handkerchief instead of curtains.

12. **(A)** 13. **(D)**

14. **(D) :** Dirt and germs collect in long nails and enter our mouth with food that we eat. Dirty hands also carry germs. These germs when enter our body, cause diseases. This is why Ramesh falls ill frequently in spite of taking healthy diet.

15. **(C)** 16. **(B)** 17. **(D)**

18. **(B) :** 'd' - Do not touch stoves, heaters, toasters or electric fan when they are switched on. They could be dangerous and cause electric shock.
'e' - At school, stand in queue.
'f' - Cross the road when the traffic light is red for vehicles.
'g' - Fly the kites in open fields and not on the terrace.

19. **(C) :** Helmet (which is hidden in the given word grid) is the safety tool used for all the three sports, cycling, cricket and skating. Safety tools for swimming include floats, swimming goggles, swimming cap, etc. which are not present in the word grid.

20. **(A)**

9 Transport and Communication

1. **(B)**

2. **(B) :** Helicopter and aeroplane (A) both are means of air transport. Sailboat and steamship (C) are means of water transport. Truck and bus (D) are means of land transport.

Option 'B' is an incorrect group because car is a means of land transport whereas submarine is a means of water transport.

3. **(D) :** The first three options, bicycle (A), cycle rickshaw (B) and hand pulled rickshaw (C) are driven by manpower while bullock cart (D) is driven by animal power.

4. **(D)**

5. **(D) :** Verbal communication involves words while non-verbal communication involves signs and symbols.

6. **(A) :** Among the given options, bus is the fastest means of transport.

7. **(D) :** Both helicopter and hot air balloon are used for air transport.

8. **(A) :** Child is ignoring road sign (A). It indicates a railway crossing and we should not cross the railway track while the gate is closed. Closed gate indicates that the train is about to come on the track.

9. **(D)**

10. **(D) :** Television is the odd one out in the given group as other three are related to post office.

11. **(D)**

12. **(A) :** Postal Index Number or PIN or Pin code is a 6 digits long post office numbering or post code system used by Indian Post. It helps the postal staff to sort letters according to their destination more quickly and easily.

13. **(B)**

14. **(B) :** Video conferencing is a latest medium of telecommunication in which digital connection is set up between two places and both the ends can send and receive audio-visual messages.

15. **(D)**

16. **(A) :** Shopping mall is to the West of school.

17. **(D) :** The means of communication in options are television (A), e-mail (B), mobile (C) and radio (D) respectively. From the letters given in box, we can get only radio.

18. **(C) :** The road signs indicate that right turn is not allowed, hospital is present on the left, speed limit for small vehicles like car is 60 kmph and for large vehicles it is 30 kmph.

19. **(A) :** The symbols given in the options mean no parking, no left turn, school ahead and speed breakers ahead, respectively. Out of these only 'no parking' is hidden in the word grid.

20. **(C) :** The communication means in options are telephone, e-mail and video call respectively out of which only video call is hidden in the word grid.

10 Air, Water and Rocks

1. **(B)**

2. **(B) :** Conservation is a careful utilisation and protection or planned management of a natural resource like water to prevent its exploitation and extinction. As Mrs Chauhan is reusing the water, which was used to wash vegetables, to water plants, this shows she is practising water conservation.

3. **(C) :** Black gold is a term applied to coal, crude oil or petroleum which are black in colour when they come out of the ground and are worth a great deal of money.

4. **(B)**

5. **(D) :** Pond is a surface water source while the other three are groundwater sources.

6. **(A) :** Tin roofs are blown away due to the upward force exerted by the fast blowing wind (moving air) inside the house.

7. **(A)**

8. **(C) :** When wind (moving air) moves in any direction, it tends to carry or move things in that direction. The given figure shows that windsock is moving towards West. This indicates that wind is moving towards West.

9. **(B) :** Rain and dew are liquid states of water while water vapour is a gaseous state of water and snow is the solid state of water.

10. **(D)** 11. **(C)** 12. **(C)**

13. **(A) :** Talcum powder is made from talc which is the softest mineral.

14. **(B) :** Water has a property to stay at the same height level from horizontal plane in the vessels that are connected to each other irrespective of their shape.

15. **(A) :** The condensation process is involved in water cycle and is also responsible for formation of water drops on any cold surface.

16. **(B)**

17. **(D) :** Pumice is a light coloured, extremely porous rock that forms during explosive volcanic eruptions. Due to its high porosity, it can float on water until it slowly becomes waterlogged. Chalk is a soft, white, porous rock. It wears away easily when rubbed, so it is used to write on blackboard.

18. **(D) :** Option 'A' can be hot air balloon and similar things, option 'B' is tubewell, option 'C' is evaporation and option 'D' is germs. Germs are living things which when present in air make it impure.

19. **(B) :** The minerals 'X' and 'Y' are talc and diamond and objects P and Q are talcum powder and jewellery respectively.

20. **(C) :** Process 'X' is evaporation and process 'Y' is condensation. During evaporation water changes from liquid state to gaseous state.

11 Earth and Universe

1. **(A) :** Mercury is the smallest planet of our Solar System and it is nearest to the Sun.

2. **(A) :** Neptune is the outermost planet of our Solar System and is thus, farthest from the Sun.

3. **(D)**

4. **(A) :** Moon is a natural satellite that revolves around Earth. Satellites do not produce their own light. They shine by reflecting sunlight. Stars on the other hand are huge balls of fire and produce their own light.

5. **(A) :** Sun rises in the East. In the given figure, Sun is in the East direction, therefore, it is the morning time. At noon time it is right overhead in the sky. In the afternoon and evening time, the Sun comes in the West direction.

6. **(B) :** Rotation is the movement of Earth on its axis. It causes day and night.

7. **(D) :** Starting from nearest to farthest planet from Sun, the sequence of planets in our Solar System is Mercury, Venus, Earth, Mars, Jupiter, Saturn, Uranus, Neptune.

8. **(A)**

9. **(B) :** Water in the pond is not flowing, it is still. A valley is a lowland between two mountains. A dam has freshwater and ocean has salty water.

10. **(A)**

11. **(D) :** In the morning and evening time, the Sun is at eastwards and westwards respectively to the pole. The Sun rays will fall on the pole from sidewards, hence the shadows formed in morning and evening time will be the longest. As the Sun rises in the sky, from morning till noon, the shadow will decrease in size and will be minimum at noon. Similarly, from noon to evening, as Sun approaches to set, the shadow will again increase in size. Given figure 'B' represents the longest shadow, therefore, it would be 4:00 p.m. in the clock.

12. **(B) :** The part of Earth towards Sun experiences day and the part of Earth away from Sun experiences night.

13. **(B) :** Revolution of Earth in its orbit along with the axial tilt causes change of season.

14. **(D) :** A pond is a small water body, surrounded by land on all sides. Rainwater fills it with water.

15. **(A)**

16. **(C) :** Moon reflects the light of the Sun, therefore we see only that part of the Moon which is lit up by the Sun; the other part remains dark and thus is invisible to us. As the Moon revolves around Earth which itself revolves around Sun, the area of the Moon lit up by Sun changes, *i.e.*, decreases gradually and then increases again. This changes the shape of Moon visible to us but actually there is no change in Moon's shape.

17. **(D)** 18. **(B)**

19. **(A) :** A shadow is formed when an opaque (non-transparent) object falls in the way of light rays and light rays get blocked. At time 'P', the tree is blocking all the light so tree's shadow is being formed but as no light is falling on Vaishali so her shadow is not being formed. At time 'Q' the sunlight is falling on her and her shadow is being formed on the tree trunk just behind her so she cannot see her shadow. Tree's shadow is being formed on tree's backside.

20. **(D) :** Jupiter is the largest planet of our Solar System. The word Jupiter is made by three boxes 8, 10, 15 of the word chop table.

Logical Reasoning

1. **(A) :** According to the given information, the order from heaviest to lightest is,

2. **(C) :** Half an hour after 2 : 40 a.m. is 3 : 10 a.m. which is shown by the clock in option (C).

3. **(C) :** The number of circles is decreased by 1 and number of triangles is increased by 1 in each step.

4. **(A)**

Figure	Sleeping	Standing	Slanting
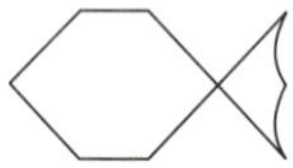	2	0	4
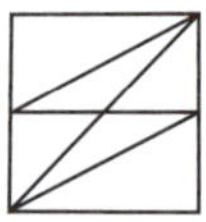	3	2	3
	2	3	2
	1	1	0
Total	8	6	9

5. **(C)**

6. **(C) :** From first figure to second, same inverted element is added above the first.

7. **(C) :** Except in option (C), in all other figures inner circle is divided into number of parts equal to number of sides of outer figure.

8. **(B) :** 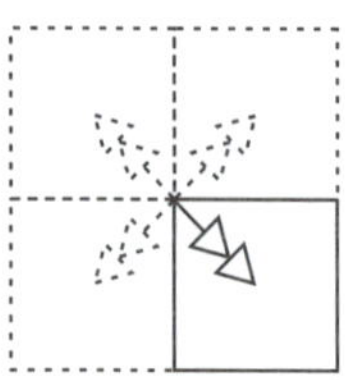

9. **(B) :** 

10. **(B)**

1 2

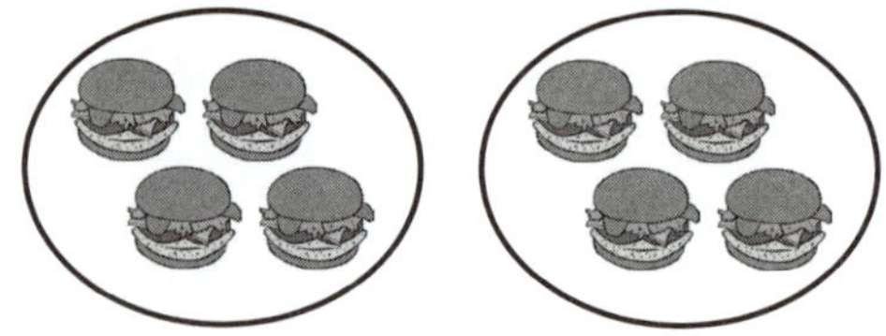

3 4

Hence, there are 4 groups of 4 burgers.

11. **(B) :**

Figure	Triangles	Circles	Squares
	1	4	2
	7	2	0
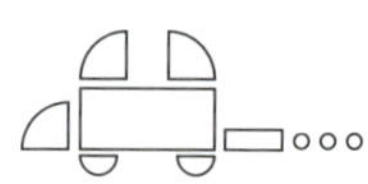	0	3	0
Total	8	9	2

Total number of both squares and triangles
= 2 + 8 = 10

So, there are 10 – 9 = 1 less circle than the triangles and squares together.

12. **(B) :** Since, number of lollipops is smallest. So, they are least likely to come out.

13. **(B)**

14. **(D) :** The pattern followed is,

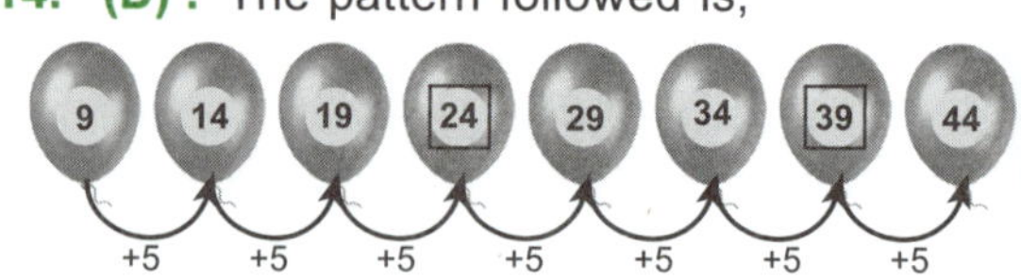

15. **(D) :** Second Tuesday of December 20XX is on 9th December. So, Pawan celebrates

his birthday on Next day of 9th December i.e., 10th December.

16. **(A) :** After interchanging, the new positions will be

So, Mohit is third from the right end.

17. **(B)**

18. **(D) :** Second element depicts the number of sides of first element.

19. **(C) :**

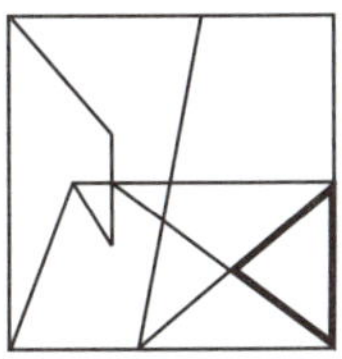

20. **(B) :** The statue is 6  tall.

21. **(C) :** King of fruits is Mango but Mango is called Orange.

22. **(C) :** Length of flower = 8 cm
Length of key = 6 – 2 = 4 cm
Length of rod = 13 – 4 = 9 cm
Length of comb = 8 – 1 = 7 cm
∴ Rod is the longest object.

23. **(D) :** Rule followed is :
Element in first row = Element in second row + 5
∴ Q = 10 + 5 = 15 and 70 = P + 5
⇒ P = 65

24. **(A) :** Straight lines are L_1, L_2 and L_3.
∴ Number of straight lines = 3
Curved lines are C_1, C_2, C_3, C_4 and C_5

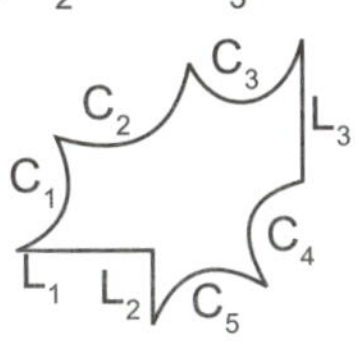

∴ Number of curved lines = 5

25. **(A) :** After interchanging, new positions of children will be

∴ R will be sixth from the left end.

26. **(A) :**  can fly but  means .

27. **(C) :** Shape (X) belongs to both groups P and R.

28. **(A) :**
Number of caps in pattern 1 = 1
Number of caps in pattern 2 = 4 = 1+3
Number of caps in pattern 3 = 7 = 4+3
∴ Number of caps in pattern 4 = 7 + 3 = 10
So, number of caps in pattern 5 = 10 + 3 = 13

29. **(B) :** Order from tallest to shortest is, Monika, Sanchi, Sandhya, Anamika.

30. **(B)**

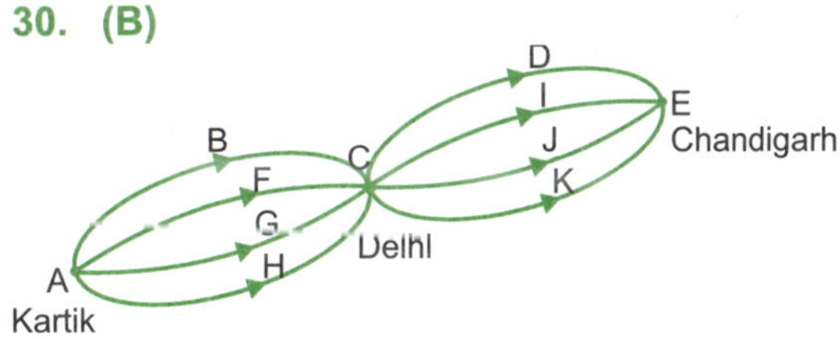

Possible ways are ABCDE, ABCIE, ABCJE, ABCKE, AFCDE, AFCIE, AFCJE, AFCKE, AGCDE, AGCIE, AGCJE, AGCKE, AHCDE, AHCIE, AHCJE, AHCKE.
∴ Number of possible ways = 16

31. **(D)**

32. **(B) :** Rectangle is missing in the given figure.

33. **(C) :** Latika is sitting between Shalini and Akansha.

34. **(D) :** MON KEY So, ORA NGE

KEY MON NGE ORA

35. **(A)**

1. **(B)**

2. **(B) :** Except Monkey in option (B), all are having banana in his hand.

3. **(C) :** 6th day after 10th October is 16th October. So, Sidak will be celebrate her birthday on 16th October.

4. **(C)**

5. **(B) :** Number of burgers in pattern 1 = 2
Number of burgers in pattern 2 = 5 = 2 + 3
Number of burgers in pattern 3 = 8 = 5 + 3
∴ Number of burgers in pattern 4 = 8 + 3
= 11
So, number of burgers in pattern 5 = 11 + 3
= 14

6. **(C) :** In group (A) tomato is the odd member as seeds of kidney beans and pea are edible but fruit of tomato is edible. In group (B) fruits of brinjal and pumpkin are edible whereas we eat root of turnip so it is the odd member. Similarly in group (D) radish is the odd member as here root is the edible part whereas we eat modified stems of potato and ginger. In group (C), sugarcane is the odd member as its stem gives sweet juice whereas in cabbage and lettuce, leaves are edible. Hence, in group (C) the odd member is incorrectly encircled.

7. **(A)**

8. **(B) :** Option (B) on unscrambling gives KENNEL which is the home of dog whereas the animal shown in the picture is cow. SHED (option A) is the place where cow is kept. Cow gives us MILK (option C) to drink. Young one of cow is called CALF (option D).

9. **(A) :** Watermelon (A) is a creeper whereas hibiscus (B), basil (C) and rose (D) are shrubs.

10. **(D)**

11. **(D) :** All insects lay eggs and have six legs. Head louse (D) is a wingless insect. So it cannot fly. Mosquito (B) and housefly (C) are winged insects so they can fly. Spider (A) is not an insect. It has eight legs. It does not have wings so it also cannot fly.

12. **(C) :** All living things breathe and need food to stay alive. Living things can move on their own.

13. **(A) :** Rice and potato are energy giving foods, milk and soybean are body building foods whereas fruits and vegetables are protective foods.

14. **(A) :** Heart (A) is the muscular pumping organ of our body which pumps oxygen rich blood from lungs to all body parts. If there is some problem in working of heart then oxygen does not reach properly to all body parts and the person feels tired.

15. **(B)**

16. **(C) :** Stilt houses are houses raised on poles over the ground. They are built primarily as a protection against flooding and are commonly found in areas where it rains heavily and floods are of common occurrence.

17. **(A) :** According to the weather forecast, it is a warm day. We preferably wear cotton clothes on warm days made of fibres obtained from cotton plant.

18. **(A)**

19. **(B) :** The given picture shows that windsock is moving towards West direction which indicates that wind is blowing towards West direction. If we want to fly a kite we should fly it in wind's direction. So, Manu should fly the kite in West direction.

20. **(B)**

21. **(B) :** Items like bread, butter, eggs, cup cakes etc, are easily available at bakery. We get medicines from chemist shop.

22. **(C) :** The given picture shows that the shadow of the object is longer than the object and is in the West direction. It means that light is falling on the object from East direction as shadows are always formed in

opposite direction of the light source. Sun is in the East direction in morning. So, it is morning time.

23. **(B) :** The given picture is of bathroom. Option B on unscrambling gives BUCKET which can be present in bathroom. OVEN (A) and TOASTER (C) are found in kitchen and PILLOW (D) is present in bedroom.

24. **(C) :** The word given in bold in the statement is 'WOOLLEN'.

25. **(D) :** We should never eat food from outside vendors as it is unhygienic and may carry germs. Eating such food can make us ill.

26. **(C) :** If any of our friends gets hurt while playing then we should not panic. Infact, we should call any adult for help.

27. **(A)** 28. **(B)** 29. **(C)**

30. **(B) :** Water in pond is not flowing, it is still. Valley is a low land between two mountains or hills. Dam is a barrier constructed across rivers (freshwater source) to control the flow and raise the level of water. Water present in oceans is salty.

31. **(B) :** According to the family tree of Sudha and Ramesh, Sudha has two grand- daughters, Surabhi and Anya. Jaya is sister of Sudhir and Ashish and sister-in-law of Deepti. Surabhi is first cousin of Anya and Avi.

32. **(B) :** In the given figure of water cycle, process 'P' is evaporation, 'Q' is condensation and R is precipitation (rainfall). Condensation (Q) is necessary for formation of clouds. By this process water vapours present in air convert into huge collection of water droplets called clouds which fall down as rain. Hence, in water cycle process P is followed by process Q which in turn is followed by process R and all these processes are necessary for completion of water cycle.

33. **(C) :** The given picture shows different land masses with places P, Q, R and S. The land masses of Earth are separated by huge water bodies called oceans.
If we want to travel from one landmass to another we can use both water transport (ship) or air transport (aeroplane).

34. **(C) :** As we can see from the table that the length of the shadow of pole Q at 7.00 a.m. and 4.00 p.m. is double than the length of shadow of pole P. So, we can conclude that the length of pole Q is double than the length of pole P. Since, the length of pole P is 2 m, the length of pole Q is 4 m.

35. **(C) :** Four professionals are hidden in the given word grid. These are tailor, farmer, barber and plumber.
All these professionals require only skills for their work and not high education.

☺☺☺

SAMPLE OMR ANSWER SHEET

1. NAME (IN ENGLISH CAPITAL LETTERS ONLY)

2. FATHER'S NAME (IN ENGLISH CAPITAL LETTERS ONLY)

Invigilator please ensure that the students write and darken the respective circles completely for School Code, Class and Roll No. columns, otherwise their Answer Sheets may not be evaluated.

3. SCHOOL CODE

Ⓐ–Ⓩ	Ⓐ–Ⓩ	⓪–⑨	⓪–⑨	⓪–⑨	⓪–⑨

4. % of Marks | **Grade**

In Last Class

Percentage OR Grade

⓪–⑨	⓪–⑨	⓪–⑨	Ⓐ–Ⓙ

5. CLASS

⓪ ① ②	⓪–⑨ Ⓜ Ⓑ

6. ROLL NO.

⓪–⑨	⓪–⑨	⓪–⑨

7. GENDER

MALE ○

FEMALE ○

8. STREAM (Only for Class XI and XII Students)

MATHEMATICS ○

BIOLOGY ○

9. MARK YOUR ANSWERS WITH HB PENCIL/BALL POINT PEN (BLUE/BLACK)

1.	Ⓐ	Ⓑ	Ⓒ	Ⓓ	19.	Ⓐ	Ⓑ	Ⓒ	Ⓓ
2.	Ⓐ	Ⓑ	Ⓒ	Ⓓ	20.	Ⓐ	Ⓑ	Ⓒ	Ⓓ
3.	Ⓐ	Ⓑ	Ⓒ	Ⓓ	21.	Ⓐ	Ⓑ	Ⓒ	Ⓓ
4.	Ⓐ	Ⓑ	Ⓒ	Ⓓ	22.	Ⓐ	Ⓑ	Ⓒ	Ⓓ
5.	Ⓐ	Ⓑ	Ⓒ	Ⓓ	23.	Ⓐ	Ⓑ	Ⓒ	Ⓓ
6.	Ⓐ	Ⓑ	Ⓒ	Ⓓ	24.	Ⓐ	Ⓑ	Ⓒ	Ⓓ
7.	Ⓐ	Ⓑ	Ⓒ	Ⓓ	25.	Ⓐ	Ⓑ	Ⓒ	Ⓓ
8.	Ⓐ	Ⓑ	Ⓒ	Ⓓ	26.	Ⓐ	Ⓑ	Ⓒ	Ⓓ
9.	Ⓐ	Ⓑ	Ⓒ	Ⓓ	27.	Ⓐ	Ⓑ	Ⓒ	Ⓓ
10.	Ⓐ	Ⓑ	Ⓒ	Ⓓ	28.	Ⓐ	Ⓑ	Ⓒ	Ⓓ
11.	Ⓐ	Ⓑ	Ⓒ	Ⓓ	29.	Ⓐ	Ⓑ	Ⓒ	Ⓓ
12.	Ⓐ	Ⓑ	Ⓒ	Ⓓ	30.	Ⓐ	Ⓑ	Ⓒ	Ⓓ
13.	Ⓐ	Ⓑ	Ⓒ	Ⓓ	31.	Ⓐ	Ⓑ	Ⓒ	Ⓓ
14.	Ⓐ	Ⓑ	Ⓒ	Ⓓ	32.	Ⓐ	Ⓑ	Ⓒ	Ⓓ
15.	Ⓐ	Ⓑ	Ⓒ	Ⓓ	33.	Ⓐ	Ⓑ	Ⓒ	Ⓓ
16.	Ⓐ	Ⓑ	Ⓒ	Ⓓ	34.	Ⓐ	Ⓑ	Ⓒ	Ⓓ
17.	Ⓐ	Ⓑ	Ⓒ	Ⓓ	35.	Ⓐ	Ⓑ	Ⓒ	Ⓓ
18.	Ⓐ	Ⓑ	Ⓒ	Ⓓ					